DEVELOPING ACCESSIBLE WEB INTERFACES

A Comprehensive Guide for Developers

DEVELOPING ACCESSIBLE WEB INTERFACES

A Comprehensive Guide for Developers

by

Gagandeep Balan, Samarth Bora

Wordpen Academics
Publishing Science That Matter

ISBN: 978-93-6084-101-0 (Hardback)

Published by : **WORDPEN ACADEMICS**
4736/23, Ansari Road, Darya Ganj,
New Delhi – 110 002
Phone: +91-011-35004336
E-mail: info@wordpenacademics.com

Printed at : **Replika Press Pvt. Ltd.**

Exclusive Distributor: ***Bio-Green Books, New Delhi***

Preface

"Developing Accessible Web Interfaces: A Comprehensive Guide for Developers" serves as an indispensable resource for web developers committed to creating inclusive digital experiences that cater to users of all abilities. This book is a culmination of best practices, practical strategies, and technical insights aimed at empowering developers to design and implement accessible web interfaces with confidence and proficiency.

In today's digital age, the web serves as a gateway to information, services, and opportunities, shaping the way we work, learn, and connect with the world. However, for individuals with disabilities, navigating the digital landscape can pose significant challenges, as barriers such as inaccessible interfaces, complex navigation, and non-standardized content hinder their ability to fully engage with online resources.

As editors of this volume, we recognize the critical importance of accessibility in ensuring equal access and participation for all users, regardless of their abilities or disabilities. Through a comprehensive exploration of accessibility principles, guidelines, and techniques, this book equips developers with the knowledge and skills needed to create web interfaces that are perceivable, operable, understandable, and robust for users of diverse abilities.

Our overarching goal in presenting this book is to foster a culture of inclusivity and empathy within the web development community, inspiring developers to prioritize accessibility as an integral aspect of their design and development process. By providing practical guidance, real-world examples, and best practices, we aim to empower developers to champion accessibility and create digital experiences that leave no one behind.

We extend our sincere gratitude to all the contributors who have generously shared their expertise, experiences, and insights in the field of accessible web development. It is our hope that this volume will serve as a catalyst for positive change, driving forward the movement towards a more inclusive and accessible web for all.

Gagandeep Balan, Samarth Bora

Contents

1

Introduction

Submitting Coding Assignments and Using GitHub

Note: If you are here as part of a course, please read on. Otherwise, submitting coding assignments is not required.

Most assignments that follow are various inaccessible web page widgets that we will ask you to make accessible by rewriting their code (HTML, CSS, or JavaScript). If you are participating here as part of a course, you will need the link to a live web page with your solution. Before the code is reviewed, the page will be checked for accessibility (using ChromeVox and other tools).

It is your decision where you want to host the pages that you will submit for review. If you have your own domain and server space, you can upload completed assignments there and submit the URL. Another option is to submit the URL of a file on GitHub to GitHack (https://raw.githack.com), then submit the URL to the output it generates as your assignment submission.

Feel free to download the activity files from our repository now, or if you are going to use GitHub, keep reading for instructions on how to fork it to your own account.

If you don't have a website, we recommend using GitHub as your platform for submitting assignments. Below we describe GitHub and GitHub Pages. If you are familiar with using GitHub or you have your own web server, you can skip the rest of this page or just scan it.

Set Up a GitHub Account

If you do not already have one, you should create a GitHub account. For any developer, it is an invaluable tool for sharing and collaborating on code development. A GitHub account is free. Though you can download the activity files from GitHub, then unzip them and work from a local directory on your hard drive, we recommend creating a fork of the activity files to your own account and cloning your fork into a local directory. Follow the link below to set up an account, then read on.

Toolkit: Join GitHub

Set Up a Local Git Environment

Depending on the operating system you are using, there are specific versions of Git for each platform. You may choose to use a Git client, or you may choose to use Git from the command line. Here we will present command line options. If you choose to use a client, see the documentation associated with the client for details on cloning, committing, pulling, and pushing.

For Windows and Mac users, if you are going to use a client instead of working from a command line, we suggest installing SourceTree. GitHub Desktop is a good alternative if you prefer to use an open source client. Feel free to choose another Git client if you like.

Toolkit: Download SourceTree or GitHub Desktop if you need a desktop Git client application.

For Linux users you can use your system's package manager to install Git for command line use. On Ubuntu, for instance, at the command prompt you can run apt-get as the root user to install Git:

```
#> sudo apt-get install git
```

Suggested Reading: For more about Git setup on Ubuntu see the tutorial on DigitalOcean.

If you are using another Linux distribution, use Google to find details on installing Git on your version of Linux.

Suggested Reading: For details on installing Git, see the Git Book.

Assignment Submissions via GitHub

Most of the assignments that follow require submitting a URL to a publicly accessible version of the widgets that are the focus of the activities.

If you need a place to post your activity assignments, GitHub Pages can be a good option. Or, you may just prefer to use GitHub Pages to organize your files so they are not cluttering your web server. You will create a fork of the activity files (learnaria.github.io), rename the repository to create your own version, and either upload it to a site of your choosing or use GitHub Pages. The GitHub Pages option is outlined here.

Suggested Reading: Using GitHub Pages.

If you choose to use GitHub Pages, follow these steps to create a copy of the files under your own GitHub account.

- Logged into GitHub, find your way to the activity files, and fork that repository. The fork button is at the top right of the GitHub screen while viewing a repository. This creates a copy of the repository under your own GitHub account where you will work from.
- After you have forked the activity files, go into the settings for that repository and change the name from learnaria.github.io to [username].github.io, where username is your GitHub account username. This will automatically create your GitHub Pages website at https://[username].github.io.
- Now you will want to create a clone of your forked activity files repository on your computer, through which you will do your work. From the command line issue the following command to create a clone of the forked version of the activity files you created, where [username] is your GitHub account username. You can also copy the https link from a field that opens when you click on the "Clone or download" button in your repo. #>git clone
- If you are using SourceTree, click on "+ New Repository" and choose "Clone from URL" and enter the above URL into the "Source URL" field. Set the "Destination Path" to your preferred work directory.

Suggested Reading: Cloning a repository.

You should now have a copy of the activity files available locally that you can edit and commit back as your assignment updates, which become part of your GitHub Pages website.

Note that it can take a few seconds or a minute for changes committed to your GitHub Pages repository to actually show up on the website.

If You Already Have a GitHub Pages Site

To add the files to an existing GitHub Pages site, open the settings for the forked repository you created. In the GitHub Pages section shown in the screenshot below, choose the Source (typically, the master branch) and click Save. This will create a subdirectory under your existing GitHub Pages site with the name of the forked repository (i.e., learnaria.github.io).

You may want to rename the repository to something shorter (e.g., learnaria) before enabling it in GitHub Pages. This would produce a URL to the activity files, something like:

https://[username].github.io/learnaria/

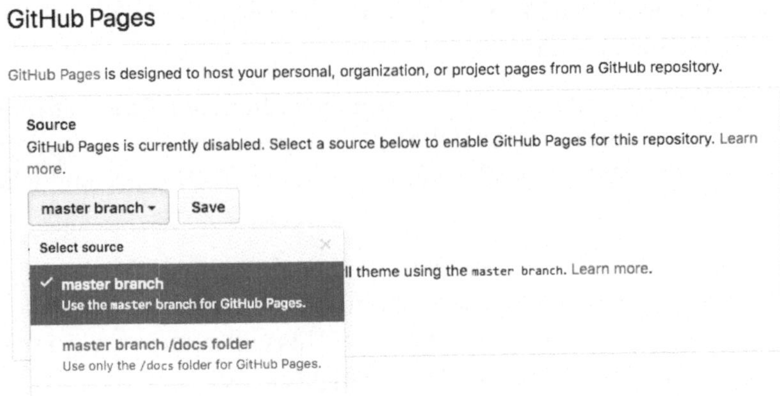

Figure: A screenshot of the GitHub Pages settings

Basic Git Commands

You do not need to be an expert Git user, but you should know a few basic commands if you are working from a command prompt. The commands you'll likely use are the following:

git status (displays a list of changed and untracked files)

git add [filename] (prepares a files for committing)

git commit -m "[message]" (describe the nature of the commit)

git push [origin master] (sends the committed change to your GitHub repository master branch)

git diff [filename] (shows the changes in a file)

Of course there are many other potential commands, but these are the most common. If you are using a Git client, such as SourceTree, these commands will be clickable in the UI buttons and menus. For more about using Git from the command line, see the Git Book.

Suggested Reading: The Git Book.

What the Activity Files Look Like

Here is what to expect once you have successfully set up the activity files. You'll note that the widgets are inaccessible. Your job throughout the activities will be to fix the accessibility of each widget.

Activity 1: How to Submit Assignments

How to Submit Assignments

If you are submitting assignments, the first task is to get setup to submit them. This can be done through GitHub Pages (recommended), another public location on the Web, or on GitHack.

Refer back to Using GitHub for details on setting up GitHub Pages.

Alternatives to GitHub Pages

- ❖ If you choose not to use GitHub Pages for your assignments, submit the URL to the index.html file of your copy of the activity files at an alternate location where you have set up your files.
- ❖ Or, submit the URL to the index.html file of your GitHub repository generated through raw.githack.com.

Requirements

If you are taking a moderated course, your instructor will provide information on how and where to submit the URLs to your various assignment submissions.

Grading Rubric

Criteria	Points
URL to Course Files: URL submitted to your copy of all the course files either in GitHub Pages or on a web server of your choosing.	10.0 pts
Total Points:	10.0

Introduction to the jQuery Plugin

Though we have chosen to focus around jQuery, much of what you'll learn here will be applicable to JavaScript in general and to other JavaScript frameworks you may be using in your work. Much of the effort here will be on creating device independent code (works with keyboard and mouse) and using script to inject WAI-ARIA into HTML as needed to dynamically manage roles, states, and properties of various interactive widgets and applications you'll be introduced to.

Throughout the activities you will be building a jQuery-ARIA plugin. We will first provide some background in the first few units, then introduce static WAI-ARIA, then move into building the plugin in Unit 4 and onward.

As you go through the activities you will be building pieces of the library one widget at a time. At the end of the activities, when you have submitted all of the assignments, we will provide you with a link to the full library that you can continue to use and build upon.

Disclaimer

When creating the activities and building the jQuery plugin, we have optimized plugin widgets to work with ChromeVox, the screen reader you'll be introduced to shortly. You may find some inconsistencies in functionality and presentation when using NVDA or JAWS (i.e., other screen readers). Compatibility or limitations across screen readers will be discussed as they come up.

Other WAI-ARIA Libraries

Though we'll focus on using the open source WAI-ARIA jQuery library we have created for the activities here, there are a couple other resources you can review that provide similar capabilities.

Toolkit: jQuery UI Accessibility Enhancements. Developed by Hans Hillen at the Paciello Group.

Toolkit: Accessible MooTools Widgets. Developed by Fraunhofer as part of an AEGIS project (no longer available through the creator).

The above libraries have been pulled apart and set up as individual demos. These demos can be found through The Chang School's Distance Education website, as part of a set of resources for a local workshop run at the university.

Toolkit: WAI-ARIA Workshop Resources

Another great resource for WAI-ARIA code and examples is the W3C's WAI-ARIA Authoring Practices site. Within the documentation are many demonstrations of how WAI-ARIA can be used. We will typically follow the best practices recommended by W3C, though, we may vary from those on occasion when more practical solutions are possible. These variations will be documented in the code comments.

Toolkit:

- WAI-ARIA Authoring Practices 1.1
- ARIA Techniques for WCAG 2.0
- Using WAI-ARIA

ChromeVox Screen Reader Install and Setup

We introduce you to ChromeVox early on, so you'll have an opportunity to practice using the screen reader we will be using throughout the activities. It will be a key tool in your toolkit that you'll use to test your work, and it will be the tool the instructors use when marking assignments.

Though there are other more popular screen readers, like JAWS and NVDA to name a couple, for day-to-day screen reader testing, ChromeVox (particularly the ChromeVox Plugin for the Chrome web browser) is our screen reader of choice because it is simple to install and configure, easy to use, free and open source, and works across computer platforms.

Another reason ChromeVox works well for accessibility testing is its good support for WAI-ARIA. WAI-ARIA is still a relatively new technology, and, as of mid-2018, it is still being supported inconsistently across available browsers and screen readers. When developing for the Web, do use WAI-ARIA as it is intended to be used as documented in the WAI-ARIA specification and test it with ChromeVox. You will still want to test with JAWS or perhaps NVDA for production testing, as these are more likely to be used by blind users. For the activities here, however, we will only be using ChromeVox.

While a relatively small number of screen reader users currently use ChromeVox, it is a highly effective tool for developers when testing web content. Also, ChromeVox is tailored to work with features of Google Drive, so even for users of other screen readers, ChromeVox may be preferable when working with Google Docs, Sheets, and Slides, etc.

Toolkit: Visit the Chrome store while using the Chrome web browser to install the ChromeVox screen reader. It will be a key element of your Toolkit.

How to Set Up the ChromeVox Screen Reader

- Open the Chrome web browser (install Chrome, if needed).
- Type "Chromevox" into Chrome's address bar, or into Google search.

- Follow the ChromeVox link to the Chrome Web Store (the first link in the search results).
- Click the "Add to Chrome" button.
- In the dialog box that opens, click "Add extension."
- Now installed, find the ChromeVox icon near the top right of Chrome to review its options.
- In the Options, set the ChromeVox modifier key to Alt or Ctrl or both (referred to here as CVox).
- In the Options, choose your preferred voice from the Voices menu.
- Done, turn ChromeVox on or off by pressing and holding the modifier key then pressing the letter "A" twice (i.e., CVox + A + A).

If you would rather see ChromeVox installed, the video below describes how to install and begin using ChromeVox.

Video: Installing ChromeVox

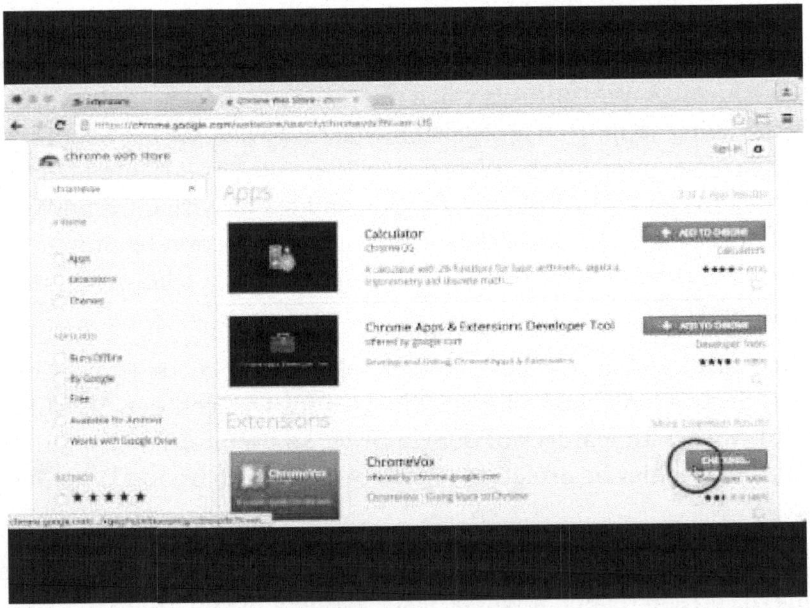

A YouTube element has been excluded from this version of the text. You can view it online here: https://pressbooks.library.ryerson.ca/wafd/?p=190

ChromeVox Testing and Associated Key Commands

Toolkit: Download the ChromeVox_Key_Commands file (Word), outlined in the table below, print it or keep it nearby when completing the first few activities.

Key Point: Be sure you have the modifier key set in ChromeVox Options, or you are going to have difficulty with the activities.

*The ChromeVox modifier key (i.e., Cvox) is set in Chrome's Settings > Extensions > ChromeVox > Options, typically set to Alt or Ctrl.

Key Point: When you are navigating with ChromeVox, it will add its own highlighting around elements when they receive focus. Test for focus visibility (WCAG 2 Guideline 2.4.7) when ChromeVox is not running. For a complete list of key commands see the ChromeVox Options, accessible through the ChromeVox button that gets added to Chrome in the top right corner of the browser during installation. Default commands are listed and can be changed if needed.

Task	Task Description	Keyboard Command
Toggle ChromeVox On/Off	To turn ChromeVox on or off without having to go into the ChromeVox Settings	Cvox+A+A
Stop Reading	Stop ChromeVox from reading	Ctrl
Default Reading	When a web page loads, ChromeVox will read the element that takes focus on the page. Use the Cvox+Arrow keys to read through content. Listen to the spoken output and note any inconsistencies from what one might expect to hear based on what is visible on the screen.	Cvox+Up and Down Arrows
Tab Navigation	When a page has loaded, press the Tab key to navigate through operable elements of the page like links and forms. Listen to the output when these elements are in focus, and note any elements that are clickable but not focusable with the keyboard. Also listen for hidden elements such as bypass links or other elements that are not visible but are read aloud by ChromeVox.	Tab, Shift + Tab
Navigate through Headings	Step through all the headings on a page. Note whether all headings are announced as expected. Note the heading level announced. Are they sequenced to create semantic structure (i.e., nested in the proper order)?	Cvox+L+H then Up/Down Arrows
Navigate through Landmarks	Step through the landmarks, key navigation points on a page. Are all areas of the page contained in a landmarked region? Note any missing landmarks.	Cvox+L+; (semi-colon) then Up/Down Arrows
List Links	List the links and navigate through them using the Arrow keys, listen for meaningfulness, or listen for context when links are otherwise meaningless.	Cvox+L+L then Up/Down Arrows

Task	Task Description	Keyboard Command
Navigate through Forms	Navigate to forms on a page, then press the Tab or F keys to listen to each of the fields. Are fields announced effectively, including required fields?	Cvox+L+F then Up/Down Arrows
Navigate through Tables	Navigate to Tables on a page, press Enter to go to a table, press Up/Down Arrow keys to move through cells in sequence (left to right, top to bottom), press Ctrl+Alt+Arrow to move to adjacent cells, press Ctrl+Alt and 5 on the number pad to list column and row headers where applicable. Note whether header cells are read or not. Are Fieldset labels announced, where applicable?	Cvox+L+T then Up/Down Arrows then Enter to select Table Cvox+Arrow to move within table Cvox+TH to announce headers

Activity 2: Set Up and Use ChromeVox

Set Up and Use ChromeVox

Key Point:

- If you are blind and use a screen reader other than ChromeVox, complete the activity using your preferred screen reader. Be sure to state the name of the screen reader you are using.
- If you are not blind, regardless of whether you use another screen reader to test accessibility for instance, please use ChromeVox. What's important is how ChromeVox interacts with the activity files you will be updating in the activities.

In this activity, you will navigate through a website using only a keyboard. Describe how the screen reader behaves. For a challenge, navigate with your monitor turned off (or darkened so you can't see what you are doing). The aim of this exercise is to discover how WAI-ARIA is making elements on the page understandable by listening alone, and to introduce screen reader review into your website testing regimen.

Refer back to ChromeVox Screen Reader Install and Setup and set up ChromeVox, if you have not already.

Requirements

Open the Web Accessibility Auditing Showcase website.

Navigate the homepage only with your monitor darkened and without using your mouse. Describe what the screen reader announces as you pass through the following elements:

- ❖ Left side menu
- ❖ Carousel at the top of the content area of the page
- ❖ Accordion on the right
- ❖ Tab panel in the centre of the page
- ❖ Landmarks present on the page (list them)

Also, answer the following questions:

- ❖ Are you able to navigate effectively?
- ❖ What difficulties did you experience, if any?
- ❖ What could be improved, if anything, to make navigation more effective?

Grading Rubric

Criteria	Points
Good descriptions provided for each element listed	5.0 pts
Three questions answered effectively	5.0 pts
Total Points:	10.0

WAI-ARIA and HTML 5

WAI-ARIA was released as a complement to HTML5. Its main purpose is to give developers more freedom to build custom web content, web applications, and interface controls created with HTML, JavaScript, and Ajax. WAI-ARIA provides a framework for adding semantics that make it possible for assistive technology users to understand and operate these custom elements.

Most HTML has built-in semantics and does not generally need WAI-ARIA. However, when HTML is being used in a non-standard way, like making a button out of a <div>, then WAI-ARIA can be added to that <div> to make it appear as a button to a screen reader by adding the following: Add the role of "button" (i.e., role="button"), add a null tabindex value (i.e., tabindex="0"), which makes it focusable, then define its state using the aria-pressed attribute, which is updated with JavaScript when the button is pressed. In the case of an actual <button> element, these properties are all already defined, so there is no need to use WAI-ARIA.

```
<div role="button" aria-pressed="false" tabindex="0">Press Me</div>
```

Though WAI-ARIA is typically used with HTML5, it can also be used with XHTML and HTML4. You may find, however, that HTML validators see WAI-ARIA as broken markup in older versions of HTML, but don't worry about that. Any WAI-ARIA related errors that a validator might identify in older HTML can generally be ignored (assuming it has been used correctly). By now though, you should be using HTML5. If you are retrofitting older code, then go ahead and add WAI-ARIA to it. If you are developing something new, then go with HTML5.

Self-Test 1

Complete the following questions to test your understanding of some key lessons in the Introduction and Unit 1.

2

Introduction to WAI-ARIA

What is WAI-ARIA?

W3C definition of WAI-ARIA

"WAI-ARIA provides a framework for adding attributes to identify features for user interaction, how they relate to each other, and their current state."

Source: W3C

WAI-ARIA provides web authors with the following:

- Roles to describe the type of widget presented, such as "menu", "treeitem", "slider", and "progressmeter"
- Roles to describe the structure of the web page, such as headings, regions, and tables (grids)
- Properties to describe the state widgets are in, such as "checked" for a check box, or "haspopup" for a menu.
- Properties to define live regions of a page that are likely to get updates (such as stock quotes), as well as an interruption policy for those updates — for example, critical updates may be presented in an alert dialog box and incidental updates occur within the page
- Properties for drag-and-drop that describe drag sources and drop targets
- A way to provide keyboard navigation for the web objects and events, such as those mentioned above

Source: W3C

Some elements of the framework can be used on their own to add accessibility to web content (e.g., landmarks). More often, they are combined with scripting that is used to dynamically add or remove WAI-ARIA attributes depending on the context.

WAI-ARIA provides semantics for custom widgets and web applications that can be understood by assistive technologies (ATs) and conveyed to users in a "human understandable" form. For example, HTML list markup might be used to create a navigation bar with menus and submenus. Without WAI-ARIA a screen reader would simply recognize the navigation bar as a collection of nested lists. Adding WAI-ARIA menu attributes (e.g., menubar, menu, menuitem, aria-haspopup, aria-expanded) can give the nested list a whole new meaning, more easily understood as a means of navigation than the list would be understood.

W3C definition of semantics

"The meaning of something as understood by a human, defined in a way that computers can process a representation of an object, such as elements and attributes, and reliably represent the object in a way that various humans will achieve a mutually consistent understanding of the object."

Source: W3C

This definition of semantics in programming is much like the common definition of the word: "the meaning, or an interpretation of the meaning" (dictionary.com). Semantics in the context of web accessibility refers to the defining of meaning as it applies to functional elements of web content, and how that functionality is conveyed to assistive technology users, especially, screen reader users.

When and When Not to Use WAI-ARIA

WAI-ARIA is supposed to be used when semantics are required to make a web application or widget understandable. For example, if you are using a <div> to create a checkbox, along with some scripting you can assign the WAI-ARIA role "checkbox" to that <div> to make it appear as a checkbox.

That said though, when there is a native HTML element available, like a checkbox, it is almost always better to use the native version than creating your own. The native version will already have all the associated semantics by default. Since the native versions are standardized, they are more likely to be supported across browsers and assistive technologies.

For native HTML elements, it is not necessary to use WAI-ARIA. For an HTML <form> element for instance, there is no need to include role="form" with the element. There are a few exceptions to this rule, however. For some of the newer HTML5 elements, like <nav> and <main> for instance, it does not hurt to include the WAI-ARIA equivalent role="navigation" and role="main" in these elements for the time being, to accommodate some of the inconsistent support for these elements across browsers and ATs. HTML validators will still give you warnings about the redundant roles, but you can safely ignore these.

You should also be careful when using WAI-ARIA with HTML elements that already have semantics. For example, if you use <h3 role="button">something</h3>, the semantics associated with the heading will be overridden, thus, potentially breaking the structure of a document. In a case like this, a better approach would be to wrap the heading in a <div> then assign role="button" to the <div> to preserve the structural semantics of the heading, as seen in the examples below.

Roles, States, and Properties

The semantics described earlier are created by adding roles, states, and properties to HTML elements.

Roles

W3C definition of roles

"Main indicator of type. This semantic association allows tools to present and support interaction with the object in a manner that is consistent with user expectations about other objects of that type."

Source: W3C

Examples of roles include menu, alert, banner, tree, tabpanel, textbox, and so on. Once assigned to an element, roles must not change over time or with user input. If, for instance, you wanted to change from a "menubar" while viewing in full screen mode to a toggle "menu" when viewed on a mobile device, the entire block of markup would change, rather than switching menubar for menu.

Roles are categorized into six groupings. Here are the groups with a few examples of each type:

- ❖ Abstract role (not to be used by authors in content, the base for the WAI-ARIA ontology)
- ❖ Widget roles (e.g., button, link, menuitem)
- ❖ Document structure roles (e.g., article, feed, list, table)
- ❖ Landmark roles (e.g., banner, navigation, main, complementary)
- ❖ Live region roles (e.g., alert, log, timer)
- ❖ Window roles (e.g., alertdialog, dialog)

Roles are typically added to HTML elements using the role attribute as follows. In the example below, an unordered list is given a role of menubar. Typically, this is used when creating a horizontal navigation bar across the top of a user interface. Each list item is given a role of menuitem.

Suggested Reading: Here is the full list of roles in WAI-ARIA 1.1.

States

W3C definition of states

"A state is a dynamic property expressing characteristics of an object that may change in response to user action or automated processes. States do not affect the essential nature of the object, but represent data associated with the object or user interaction possibilities. See: clarification of states versus properties."

Source: W3C

States are used along with roles, typically, to define its functional status. States are much like properties, though they typically change while an application or widget is being used (e.g., aria-checked changes between true and false). Properties typically do not change (e.g., aria-labelledby keeps the same value). States and properties are all "aria-" prefixed, unlike roles.

Here are a few examples of states:

- Aria-busy
- Aria-checked
- Aria-expanded
- Aria-disabled
- aria-hidden

Properties

W3C definition of properties

"Attributes that are essential to the nature of a given object, or that represent a data value associated with the object. A change of a property may significantly impact the meaning or presentation of an object. Certain properties (for example, aria-multiline) are less likely to change than states, but note that the frequency of change difference is not a rule. A few properties, such as aria-activedescendant, aria-valuenow, and aria-valuetext are expected to change often. See clarification of states versus properties."

Source: W3C

Properties, as mentioned above, are much like states in how they are used along with roles. However, unlike states that change, properties tend to remain the same (though this is not a rule). Intuitively, you may notice the changing nature of states listed above, and the static nature of properties listed below.

Here are a few examples of properties:

- Aria-describedby
- Aria-atomic
- Aria-autocomplete
- Aria-colcount
- Aria-colspan
- Aria-controls

Suggested Reading: See the WAI-ARIA Specification for a full list of states and properties.

Static vs. Dynamic WAI-ARIA

Even if you don't use Java Script, there is a good amount you can do with static WAI-ARIA to improve the accessibility of a website or web application. You may have already gathered from the discussion of states and properties that some WAI-ARIA can be written right into the HTML of a web page (e.g., properties and landmarks). Others need to be dynamically updated based on user input or context (e.g., states and some properties).

Some of the static WAI-ARIA attributes you are likely to use are listed below, with their descriptions from W3C.

Global Static Properties

- **Aria-describedby:** Identifies the element (or elements) that describes the object.
- **Aria-labelledby:** Identifies the element (or elements) that labels the current element.
- **Aria-label:** Defines a string value that labels the current element.
- **Aria-controls:** Identifies the element (or elements) whose contents or presence are controlled by the current element.
- **Aria-owns:** Identifies an element (or elements) in order to define a visual, functional, or contextual parent/child relationship between DOM elements where the DOM hierarchy cannot be used to represent the relationship.
- **Aria-details:** Identifies the element that provides a detailed, extended description for the object.

Below is an example of some of these attributes in action. Though this example would need some scripting to handle the submenu opening and closing, and dynamically updating aria-expanded to false when the submenu is closed, and update the active element referenced in aria-activedescendant, you can get an idea of the semantics that are being applied to make the nested list announce itself as a menu. Watch or listen to the screen reader output in the video that follows the code box below to understand how the WAI-ARIA attributes are read. Examine the code in the code box to understand what WAI-ARIA is being used to produce that output.

How Does the Above Markup Work?

- Navigating with the Tab key, focus first goes to the "menu_container" div, which is made keyboard focusable with the tabindex="0" attribute.
- There the screen reader reads the content of the "chooser" div, identified by aria-details, describing what the menu is used for. This div is hidden from view but available to screen readers. This div could be made visible to make it available for everyone.
- Next, the "offerings" UL receives focus, also made focusable with tabindex="0".
- There, the screen reader reads the content of the "navhowto" div, identified by aria-describedby, explaining how to navigate the menu. This div is hidden from view for most users.
- Next, using the Arrow keys as instructed by the "navhowto" div, the 'Home' menuitem takes focus, announcing "menubar expanded with submenu, Home, menu". Probably a little more verbose in this case than it needs to be, but that's how ChromeVox handles menu items.
- Using the Down Arrow key, focus is moved to the "Courses" menu item, announcing "Courses, menu expanded with submenu." The aria-haspopup attribute is what causes a screen reader to announce a submenu. aria-expanded="true" causes the screen reader to announce that the menu is expanded.
- Using the Down Arrow, focus moves into the submenu, announcing "Menu with two items, Economics, menuitem 1 of two." The submenu is announced as a menu of its own, identified by adding role="menu" to the UL containing the two submenu items.
- Finally, using the Down Arrow, the screen reader announces "Computer Science, menuitem two of two."

Here's a video that shows how ChromeVox would read out the menu described above:

Video: Example Menu with WAI-ARIA (0:33)

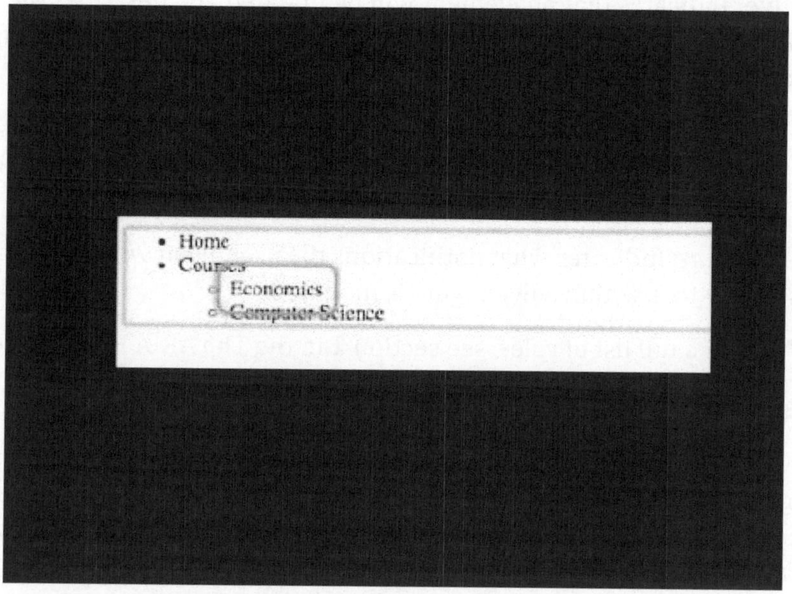

A YouTube element has been excluded from this version of the text. You can view it online here: https://pressbooks.library.ryerson.ca/wafd/?p=272

Most of the WAI-ARIA elements described in the above series of steps can be used statically by typing the attributes right into the HTML. The aria-activedescendant would typically be dynamically updated with script as the menuitems are selected. The aria-expanded would also be updated dynamically switching between true and false when the submenu is toggled opened or closed.

Here are some more static WAI-ARIA attributes, which we'll look at in a little more detail later as you complete the activities.

Widget Static Attributes

- **Aria-haspopup:** Indicates the availability and type of interactive popup element, such as menu or dialog, that can be triggered by an element.
- **Aria-modal:** Indicates whether an element is modal when displayed
- **Aria-readonly:** Indicates that the element is not editable but is otherwise operable.
- **Aria-required:** Indicates that user input is required on the element before a form may be submitted.

Live Static Regions

- **Aria-live:** Indicates that an element will be updated and describes the types of updates the user agents, assistive technologies, and user can expect from the live region.
- **Aria-atomic:** Indicates whether assistive technologies will present all, or only parts of, the changed region based on the change notifications defined by the aria-relevant attribute.
- **Aria-relevant:** Indicates what notifications the user agent will trigger when the accessibility tree within a live region is modified.

Toolkit: For a full list of roles, see section 1 in the The ARIA Role Matrices.

Browser and Screen Reader Support for WAI-ARIA

Because WAI-ARIA is relatively new, its support across browsers and assistive technologies is still somewhat inconsistent. That should not, however, discourage you from using it. Be aware that workarounds may be needed in some cases, at least for the short term as browsers and assistive technologies progress to implement support for the full WAI-ARIA specification.

For now, it is advisable to test WAI-ARIA implementations across multiple browsers and screen readers.

Look over the following references and add them to your Toolkit.

Toolkit:

- WAI-ARIA Screen Reader Compatibility (Dec 27, 2017) Note: This resource does not include ChromeVox.
- WAI-ARIA Browser Compatibility
- ARIA Alert Support
- User Agent Support Notes for ARIA Techniques

Graceful Degradation vs. Progressive Enhancement

Given the range of support for WAI-ARIA across current screen readers and browsers, strategies like graceful degradation and progressive enhancement are useful for accommodating varying implementations and ensuring that tools developed with WAI-ARIA are accessible regardless of support.

Depending on your situation, one development method may be preferable over the other, though in general progressive enhancement is preferred over graceful degradation. That is, creating base functionality that works for everyone is preferred, rather than providing enhancements when they are supported by the browser and/or assistive technology. Graceful degradation, on the other hand, starts with the enhancement, then provides alternatives where the enhancements are not supported. While they may sound equivalent, the latter typically requires less effort, even though it is more of a Band-Aid solution to correct an incompatibility. The former takes a little more effort and is more about providing enhancements when they are supported while always providing a base functionality that works for everyone.

Definitions

In his article, "Graceful degradation versus progressive enhancement," Christian Heilman provides some useful definitions that help distinguish between the two methods:

"**Graceful degradation** – Providing an alternative version of your functionality or making the user aware of shortcomings of a product as a safety measure to ensure that the product is usable."

"**Progressive enhancement** – Starting with a baseline of usable functionality, then increasing the richness of the user experience step by step by testing for support for enhancements before applying them."

"Degrading gracefully means looking back whereas enhancing progressively means looking forward whilst keeping your feet on firm ground."

Suggested Reading: These definitions come from: Graceful degradation versus progressive enhancement (Christian Heilman, CC-BY NC-SA).

When to Use Which Method with WAI-ARIA

Though progressive enhancement and graceful degradation are development methods that might be followed on any web project, here, we talk about them as they relate to the use of WAI-ARIA.

Support for WAI-ARIA is improving constantly, but there are still many inconsistencies between browsers and assistive technologies. And there will still be those using older assistive technologies that were around before WAI-ARIA support was added. Because assistive technologies tend to be expensive, users tend to upgrade less often, thus it is important to support technologies that may be five years old or somewhat older.

Browsers, on the other hand, are typically free, and readily available. However, that does not necessarily mean developers can rely on users having the latest or even a current browser. It is not uncommon, particularly in large organizations, to restrict employees' ability to upgrade their own systems.

A simple example of progressive enhancement (though it could also be seen as graceful degradation) is in within–web page navigation for screen reader and keyboard-only users. Before the advent of WAI-ARIA landmarks, the way to provide this within-page navigation was to provide bypass links, which would typically be located at the top left of the page. These bypass links lead to strategically placed anchors, often next to navigation elements and at the top of the main content area. These links are standard HTML and will work for everyone. WAI-ARIA landmarks are relatively new, though support for them in current browsers and assistive technologies is good. But, given some users will be using older technologies, at least for the short term, it is advisable to provide landmarks as an enhancement and continue using bypass links to ensure there is always a way to navigate effectively through web content.

Similarly, when using the newer HTML elements that may not be supported by current assistive technologies, it is a good idea to use redundant roles, at least in the short term. For example, <nav> and <main> are new HTML elements, which are supposed to be equivalent to the navigation and main WAI-ARIA roles. However, not all ATs support the new tags at present. Thus, it's advisable to use redundant roles with these elements, as seen in the markup below, even though HTML validators will flag them as a warning.

Validating WAI-ARIA

There are a number of tools that can be used to validate WAI-ARIA to ensure it is being used correctly. Watch the following video for a quick look at WAI-ARIA validation with Lighthouse and aXe. Install these tools in your browser, so you have them available for testing as you complete the activities in the coming units.

Video: WAI-ARIA Validation

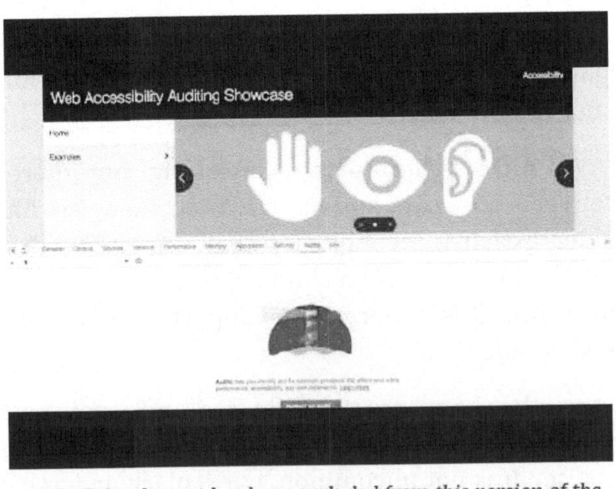

A YouTube element has been excluded from this version of the text. You can view it online here: https://pressbooks.library.ryerson.ca/wafd/?p=281

Toolkit:

Web-Based Validator

- W3C HTML Validator (validates WAI-ARIA as part of HTML5)

Chrome

- Chrome Developer Tools (comes with Chrome)
- Lighthouse (extends Chrome Developer Tools with an Audit tab)
- ARIA Validator
- aXe (for Chrome)

Firefox

- aXe (for Firefox)

WAI-ARIA Taxonomy

In addition to the full list of WAI-ARIA attributes in the specification, the visual presentation of that list in the WAI-ARIA taxonomy can be helpful in understanding the relationships between elements. This image can also help those who are visual learners to see how WAI-ARIA is organized. Click on the thumbnail below to open the full visual taxonomy.

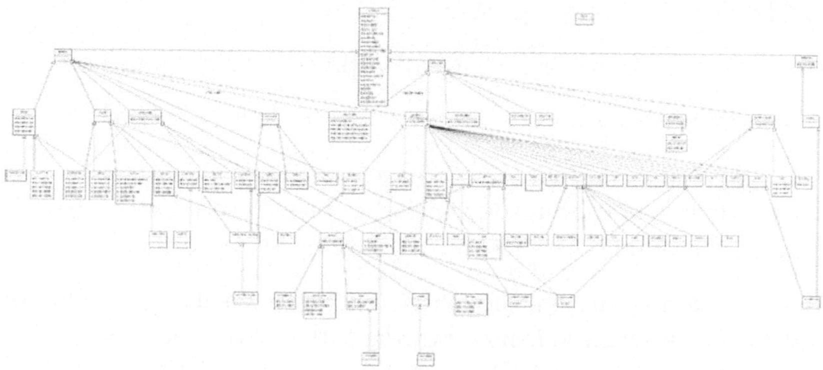

Figure: WAI-ARIA taxonomy thumbnail. Click to open full-sized image.

Also, see the SVG version of the WAI-ARIA taxonomy

A UML-XMLversion and an RDF version are also available to import into systems that support those formats.

Suggested Reading: A representation or the WAI-ARIA taxonomy as a cheat sheet.

Activity 3: WAI-ARIA Scavenger Hunt

WAI-ARIA Scavenger Hunt

The overall goal of the instruction here is to provide the tools and knowledge needed to make web interactivity accessible to screen reader users. In this activity, you will use ChromeVox and code review to identify WAI-ARIA used throughout the Web Accessibility Auditing Showcase home page.

Requirements

Although we have only touched on the details of WAI-ARIA, in this activity, you will be spending some time examining the homepage of the Web Accessibility Auditing Showcase website. Use a combination of the following to determine how the WAI-ARIA elements are being used:

- ❖ Test with ChromeVox to hear what WAI-ARIA sounds like with a screen reader.
- ❖ Review the source code.
- ❖ For full marks on this activity, list at least five static and five dynamic WAI-ARIA enabled elements in your answer. Include a brief description for each. Here's a few made-up examples of what you might report in your findings:
- ❖ Aria-describedby: used in the outer div of the side menu, to announce instructions on how the side menu works with a keyboard
- ❖ Tabindex="0": used to give keyboard access to the custom buttons in the User Survey
- ❖ Role="menu": used to make the main navigation list appear as a menu to screen readers

Finally, here is the Web Accessibility Auditing Showcase website. Review only the home page.

Key Point: There is static and dynamic WAI-ARIA used in this page. You may View Source to find any static WAI-ARIA being used. Use your browser's Inspect tool to find dynamic WAI-ARIA. Interact with the site to produce changes to the dynamic WAI-ARIA, and note those changes.

Note: Not all ARIA-related markup starts with the "aria-" prefix. Scan through the WAI-ARIA documentation introduced in this unit for a listing of all potential WAI-ARIA markup you might come across. Also, not all accessibility enhancements are WAI-ARIA. For example, alt is an accessibility feature of the HTML img element. You can mention these other accessibility features; however, they will not count toward your mark on this activity.

Grading Rubric

Criteria	Points
At least five instances of static WAI-ARIA being used in the page are listed.	5.0 pts
At least five instances of dynamic WAI-ARIA being used in the page are listed.	5.0 pts
Total Points:	10.0

Self-Test 2

Answer the following questions to test your understanding of key lessons in this unit.

3

Basic WAI-ARIA

WAI-ARIA Landmarks

WAI-ARIA landmarks are used to define regions on a web page. They provide a means for assistive technology users to effectively navigate the various areas of a page. WAI-ARIA landmarks should be used with other means of within-page navigation, such as bypass links and page headings. These two latter means of navigating have been around for much longer, and many will continue to use these elements as their primary method of moving around within a web page.

There are eight landmark roles.

Follow the links below to read about each type of landmark:

- Banner
- Complementary
- Contentinfo
- Form
- Main
- Navigation
- Region
- Search

In the following short video, you will see how ChromeVox interacts with landmarked regions for the next activity coming up in this unit. Use it as a model for implementing your own landmarks. Aim to have your activity submission operate the same as it does in the video.

Video: WAI-ARIA Landmarks Demo (1:07)

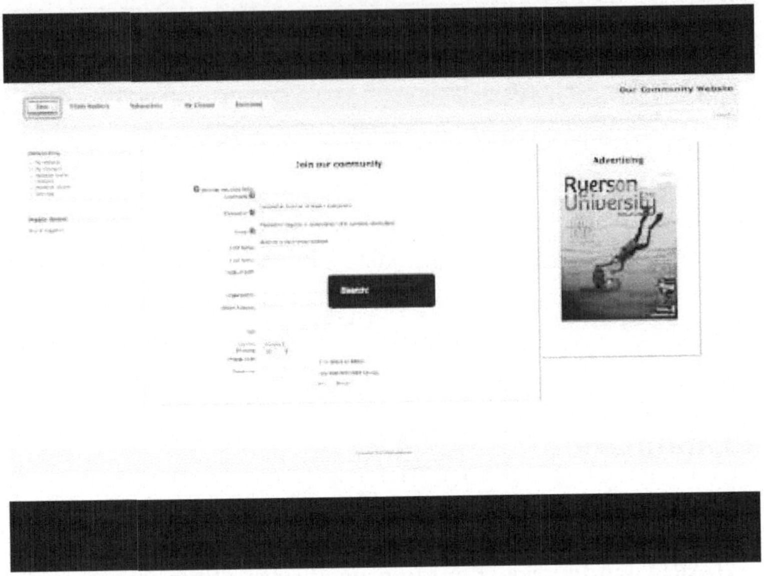

A YouTube element has been excluded from this version of the text. You can view it online here: https://pressbooks.library.ryerson.ca/wafd/?p=303

To help visualize landmarked regions, the figure below presents well-defined areas on the page, each of which serves a different purpose. Banner areas, the element that contains the content of each banner region, would be assigned role="banner". The menu on the left would have its container assigned role="navigation", as would other navigation bars or menus if they were present. The main content area, assigned role="main", is where the primary content of the page appears. There should only be one main region. The region on the right containing secondary information, assigned role="complementary", is where you might find advertising or related resources. And, finally, the container around the footer area would be assigned role="contentinfo". This is where details such as copyright, a privacy statement, contact information, etc., would be located.

Websites may be laid out in a multitude of ways; this particular layout is just an example. The landmarks assigned to any given region should reflect the function of that particular region, regardless of where it might appear on the page. If advertising were spread across a region at the bottom of the page, for example, then that region would be assigned role="complementary".

Example of landmarked regions of a web page:

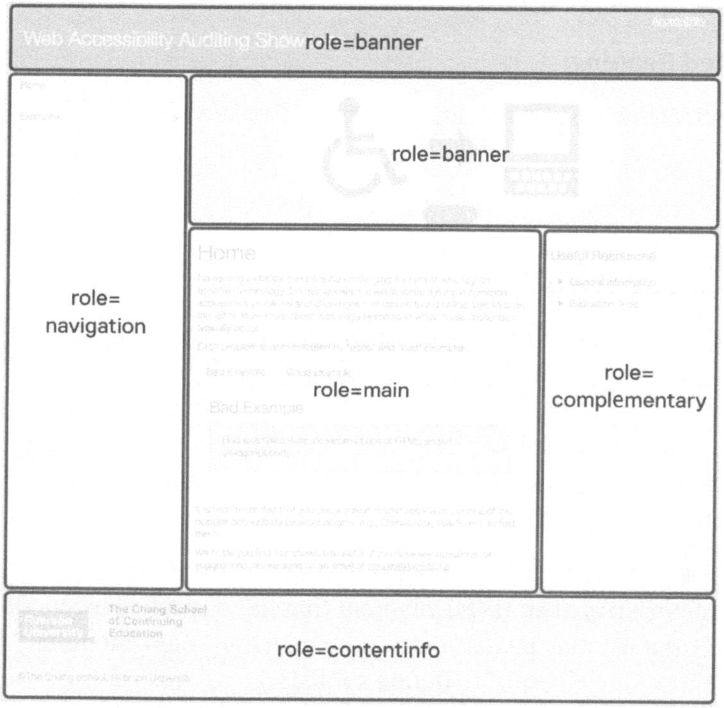

Custom Regions

While most of the landmarks are relatively self-explanatory in terms of what they should contain, role="region" needs some explanation. This landmark role can be used to contain specific information that is not effectively described by one of the other landmark roles and is important enough that a user might want to navigate directly to that area of the page. When it is used, it must be accompanied by aria-label or aria-labelledby if there is an existing element on the page that describes the region (such as a heading).

For example, you may want to define a specific area on each page where contact information or a contact form is located. The following markup might be used to define a "contact region."

Other Considerations When Using Landmarks

- **The whole page defined in regions:** When landmarks are used, it is considered best practice to contain all information presented on a page within a region, so no information is orphaned outside the defined regions.
- **Duplicate roles:** For landmarks that may be used for multiple regions, such as role="navigation", these regions should be distinguished from one another. For instance, use aria-label or aria-labelledby to describe a "main navigation"

bar and a "content menu." Both are considered navigation features, even though they serve different purposes.

Suggested Reading:

- Using ARIA landmarks to identify regions of a page
- Page Regions (WAI Web Accessibility Tutorials)
- ARIA Landmarks Example

Common Static WAI-ARIA

Much of the WAI-ARIA introduced so far is static. That is, it can be written directly into HTML elements as attributes, their values typically do not change, and they do not require scripting to control their behaviour. Landmarks and roles, for example, are all static. Anyone who knows how to read and write HTML can make use of these attributes by simply adding them to HTML elements. WAI-ARIA properties are also typically static, though not always.

As discussed earlier, static WAI-ARIA often consists of properties given to define specific characteristics of an HTML element that has a particular functional role. For example, a nested list may be defined as a menu using role="menubar" to define the top-level list and role="menu" to define sublists.

List items in the top-level list that have a nested sublist would be given the attribute aria-haspopup="true" (or aria-haspopup="menu"). Thus, when encountered by assistive technology, a list item with this attribute will announce that a submenu is present (e.g., "menu with submenu" when using ChromeVox).

Try This: Using ChromeVox, navigate through the menu bar widget example below, created by Hans Hillen at the Paciello Group, to hear how submenus are announced. Open this demo in a new window.

Frequently Used WAI-ARIA Attributes

You have already been introduced to a few static attributes. Those and a handful of others you are likely to use regularly are listed here. This is not a full list. Follow the links and read through their descriptions.

- Aria-describedby
- Aria-labelledby
- Aria-label
- Aria-required
- Aria-controls

- Aria-details
- Aria-haspopup
- Aria-live
- Aria-owns
- Aria-relevant
- Aria-roledescription

WAI-ARIA Alert and Message Dialogs

Providing feedback after a user completes an action is a critical accessibility feature. Feedback can be an error message when something has gone wrong. Additionally, it can be a confirmation or warning, after which a user has to make a decision before proceeding. Or, it could be completion feedback that is presented after a particular action has occurred to indicate it was successful.

The latter is often overlooked by developers. However, for people using a screen reader, notification that an action was successful can be as important as providing error messages. When completion feedback is provided, screen reader users do not need to search through the content of the screen to be sure the action they just completed was successful — the process can be quite time-consuming.

In each type of feedback, it is critical that messages be easy to access. The best strategy for making feedback accessible is to use the WAI-ARIA alert or alert-dialog roles. These are both types of live regions. When the content of the container element with role="alert" changes, the content that appears is automatically read aloud by screen readers. A WAI-ARIA alert has an implicit aria-live="assertive" and aria-atomic="true" (to be covered in more detail in the section on live regions). This means that, when the message appears, it will interrupt whatever the screen reader is in the middle of reading, and the entire content of the element will be read, as opposed to just the new content added (i.e., aria-atomic="false").

Try This: In the following example of a WAI-ARIA alert, start ChromeVox, then press the "Say Something" button to hear how ChromeVox handles the message that appears. Examine the script and HTML below to see how it was done.

alert vs. alertdialog

Error, warning, and completion feedback will typically be created with role="alert", while confirmation feedback will often use role="alertdialog". Use role="alert" when no user input is needed. Use role="alertdialog" when user input is expected, with focus sent to the dialog. At least one element in the dialog must be focusable when using role="alertdialog".

Watch and listen to the following video to understand how ChromeVox handles WAI-ARIA alerts.

Video: WAI-ARIA Alerts (1:09)

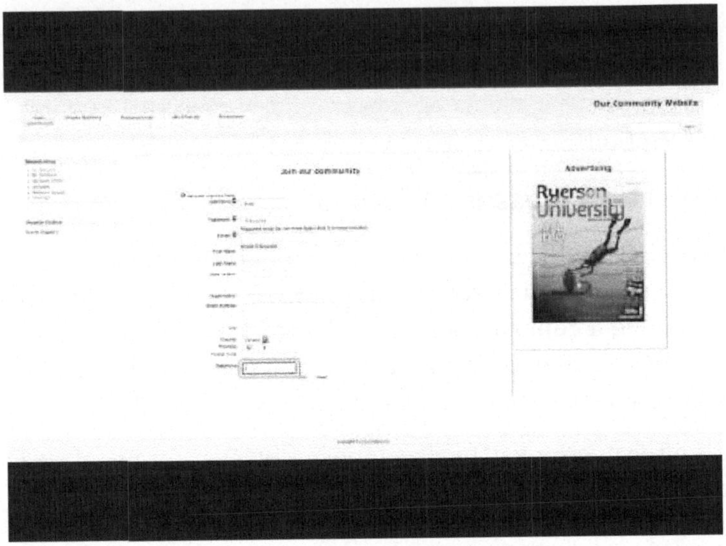

A YouTube element has been excluded from this version of the text. You can view it online here: https://pressbooks.library.ryerson.ca/wafd/?p=308

Suggested Reading: Using ARIA role="alert" or Live Regions to Identify Errors

Modal Dialogs

Modal dialogs interrupt users and require an action. They are appropriate when users' attention needs to be directed toward important information.

Modal dialogs are defined using role="alertdialog" and aria-modal="true". Be aware what WAI-ARIA is used for modals, and be aware that when a modal dialog is displayed, focus must be sent to the dialog, and it must remain in the dialog until whatever interaction is complete (e.g., clicking the confirmation button) and the dialog closes. When the dialog closes, focus must be returned to the location from where the dialog was opened.

Dialogs

Dialogs are used like modal dialogs are, except it is still possible to interact with the other content of the page. These are defined using role="dialog".

Suggested Reading:

- ❖ Using the Dialog Role (Mozilla)
- ❖ Modal and Nonmodal Dialogs: When (and When Not) to Use Them

Using Tabindex

As you may know, the HTML tabindex attribute is a way to order the path the cursor takes as users use the Tab key to navigate through a website or web application. In general, however, you want to avoid using tabindex in this way, particularly when it disrupts the default tab order, which may end up creating confusion when the cursor does not follow an expected path (i.e., left to right, top to bottom). That's not to say don't ever use them, but be careful.

With HTML5 and the introduction of WAI-ARIA, tabindex="0" is added to make it possible for developers to add keyboard accessibility to an element that would not normally have keyboard functionality. For example, it might be used to make a <div> focusable. Likewise, tabindex="-1" is added to remove keyboard accessibility from an element. The two are likely to be used with scripting to dynamically add and remove keyboard access to elements when focus needs to be strategically placed within a widget or web application. When the tabindex attribute is used in this way, it is referred to as a roving tabindex.

Try This: Take a look at the tab panels throughout the Showcase site to see how the tabs in the tabpanels toggle between values "-1" and "0" to control which tab has focus, using your browser's Inspect feature. This demo works better on a wide screen, before responsiveness kicks in. Either reduce the zoom level, or drag your browser window wider until the menu appears at the side, instead of above the content.

Open demo in a new window.

You can also use tabindex="0" in a static way when context is needed to describe how to use a menu, for instance. A <div> can be wrapped around the menu, given tabindex="0" to make it focusable, so, when a user navigates to the <div>, it announces instructions for using the keyboard to navigate within the menu. The following example demonstrates using tabindex, along with aria-label, to provide context information. If you navigate through the Showcase site above with ChromeVox, you'll notice this strategy with the side menu, announcing how to operate the menu with a keyboard.

Keyboard Interaction

Keyboard access is perhaps the most important accessibility feature that can go into a website, widget, or web application. However, it is often overlooked by developers, who are typically mouse users and may not have keyboard usability as a part of their testing regimen. People who are blind are typically unable to use a mouse, so any feature that relies on a mouse alone to function will likely be inaccessible to them. Fortunately, it is relatively easy to include keyboard access. It's more a matter of remembering to add it when mouse access is added.

The following is a simple example of including both mouse and keyboard events when defining interaction for a widget or web application. Examine the JavaScript to see how mouse and keyboard events are handled, then under the Result tab, try operating the button with a keyboard and mouse while using ChromeVox. How you go about implementing both mouse and keyboard doesn't really matter, as long as it is possible to interact with both.

You may notice some inconsistencies in ChromeVox support for the live region used to present the messages in the example, more specifically the aria-atomic attribute. Live regions will be covered more thoroughly later in this unit.

Predictability, Consistency, and Convention

Here we will introduce the basics of keyboard interaction, and we'll go into greater detail when we start looking more closely at particular widgets and design patterns as they are introduced in the units that follow.

As the heading for this section suggests, keyboard interaction needs to be predictable, consistent, and should follow convention. That is, users should have a good idea of the path that the focus will follow (predictable). When navigating with the Tab key, that path should be the same throughout an application or website (consistent). Finally, it should be like it is in other applications, websites, or operating systems (convention).

Suggested Reading: Developing a Keyboard Interface

Take for example a combo box (aka, a select menu). Regardless of the operating system being used, combo boxes work the same way. If you are developing a widget out of divs that function like a combo box, it should operate like a standard HTML combo box.

Conventional keyboard interaction for a combo box:

- Tab to navigate into the combo box
- While in focus, tab to navigate beyond the combo box
- While in focus, Shift + Tab to navigate before the combo box
- While in focus, Down Arrow to show next option
- While in focus, Up Arrow to show previous option
- While in focus, Alt + Down Arrow to display options list

- ❖ While options list is open, Alt + Up Arrow to close the options list
- ❖ While options list is open, Esc to close the options list and return to default state
- ❖ While an option is in focus, Enter to select that option

When developing a custom combobox — typically, a text box and list of options — a grid, a tree, or a dialog are combined into a functional unit that should operate like a standard HTML select menu. Functionality in addition to that described above may be added to the custom combobox, e.g., to add autocompletion. As the user types letters into the text box, options beginning with the string type are displayed below as a list or the first option with those letters is displayed inline in the text box.

Try This: Using your keyboard, try the keyboard interactions described above to confirm whether or not the combobox functions in a conventional way. Try it with a few different browsers and notice any variations in how different browsers handle combobox interaction.

Suggested Reading: For detailed discussion of combobox design patterns, see: WAI-ARIA Authoring Practices 1.1 (Combo Boxes)

Toolkit: For a list of design patterns, and keyboard interaction conventions, review the following widget development best practices. Scan for now. They will be covered more thoroughly in later units.

- ❖ Combobox
- ❖ Grid
- ❖ Listbox
- ❖ Menu or menu bar
- ❖ Radiogroup
- ❖ Tabs
- ❖ Toolbar
- ❖ Tree View

Application and Presentation Roles

The application and presentation roles in WAI-ARIA change the way assistive technologies interact with web content. Both have "use with caution" warnings. Their use and where and when to use them are described here.

Application Role

The application role is used when there is not a corresponding widget interaction pattern available to provide semantics for a custom widget.

Imagine, for instance, a file manager application embedded in a web page, which does not have widget roles specifically defined. It may have many of the functions a typical file manager might have on a Windows, Mac, or Linux system. It might have the typical File, Edit, and View menus that most applications have, including browsers. Those menus in the file manager should function like these same menus in other applications. When the application role is used in a container containing the embedded file manager, keystrokes are intercepted and repurposed to operate the file manager, instead of the browser and the assistive technology.

When in the file manager application, this behaviour may be desirable. But, defined with the application role, all of the standard screen reader shortcut keys are also disabled, so the user is no longer able to navigate the pages by headings, or landmarks, for instance, while inside the application. This may be fine in such a case because the screen reader user will likely temporarily want shortcut keys to file manager functions, and not those of the browser or screen reader.

If, however, the application role is used to contain a carousel widget, for example, then browser and assistive technology functionality may be unnecessarily disabled, potentially creating barriers. A carousel widget typically has limited functionality. For example, carousels may contain scripted Arrow keys to move back and forth between slides, between headings within each slide for added structure, or link to another section of the site presented in a slide. In such cases, screen reader users would be unable to navigate through the slides by listing headings or links, using their screen reader's default heading and link list functionality. By removing the application role, the scripted next/previous link, as well as the heading and the links could be used to navigate the carousel.

The bottom line is to use the application role carefully. Be sure it is not creating more barriers than it is intended to prevent.

Presentation Role

Much like the application role disables default keyboard functionality, the presentation role (and its synonym role="none"), theoretically, removes the default semantics from children of the element it applies to.

So, for instance, if you have a list with role="presentation", it should not announce as a list, and its list items should not announce as list items. However, nested lists within those suppressed list items will announce as usual.

There are a couple of intended exceptions where the presentation role will not remove default semantics:

- When role="presentation" is not applied to elements that have tab focus, such as links, form elements, and elements that have tabindex defined, or

- Where an element has been modified with any of the 21 global states or properties

Where role="presentation" is applied to a parent element, all of its child elements should inherit that role, but not all of its grandchildren. For example, if <ul role="presentation"> is used then the semantics for each of its <li> elements will be ignored. But, if an <li> contains a sublist, that list would be announced as usual.

It should be noted that current support for the presentation role is spotty across browsers and assistive technologies, and you are likely to find it not all that useful if you're trying to develop with cross browser compatibility. Typically, tables, images, and headings are affected by the presentation role, while other elements like lists, forms, and links are not, or only partially affected. If you are trying to hide elements completely from screen readers, you might consider using either aria-hidden or CSS display :none.

Three common uses for role="presentation" include:

- Hiding a decorative image. It is equivalent to giving the image null alt text.
- Suppressing table semantics for tables used for layout in circumstances where the table semantics do not convey meaningful relationships.
- Eliminating semantics of intervening orphan elements in the structure of a composite widget, such as a tablist, menu, or tree as demonstrated in the example above.

Source: WAI-ARIA Authoring Best Practices

There are also a number of WAI-ARIA roles that act like the presentation role, and these suppress the default semantics for the elements to which they are applied. For instance, if a tablist is created from a <ul>, and role="tab" is applied to each of the list items within that <ul>, their default listitem role will be replaced with the tab role, without the need to set them as presentational.

The following JSFiddle examples have been created for cross browser testing of the presentation role. Navigate through each example with ChromeVox + Chrome. If you have them available, also navigate them with JAWS + IE and NVDA + FF to understand the varied support for the presentation role. Below, the fiddle is a listing of support for current versions of these screen readers.

Screen Reader Output from the Above Demo

NVDA (2018.1.1) + Edge (41.16299.248.0)

By keyboard, only the link is announced. Mouseover, though, and all elements are announced.

- **Link:** not announced
- **List:** not announced or keyboard focusable
- **Headings:** not announced or keyboard focusable
- **Table:** not announced or keyboard focusable
- **Image:** not announced or keyboard focusable
- **Form:** "Combo box opt three collapsed"

NVDA (2018.1.1) + FireFox (59.0.2)

- **Link:** announces as usual
- **List:** values announced but not bullets or the list itself
- **Headings:** announce as usual
- **Table:** not announced.
- **Image:** not announced
- **Form:** announces opts but not the combobox

JAWS (18) + Edge (41.16299.248.0)

- **Link:** focusable, but not announced
- **List:** not focusable, not announced
- **Headings:** does not announce first heading, but does announce second heading
- **Table:** not announced
- **Image:** not announced
- **Form:** not focusable, not announced

ChromeVox (53.0.2784.5)

- **Link:** focusable, but not read (using Tab key) Announces as usual when using CVOX + Arrows
- **List:** Skips over list (using Arrow key) except when link receives focus first, then Arrow key announces the numbers in the list. Announces numbers but not as a list when using CVOX + Arrows
- **Headings:** Does not announce the first heading, but does announce the second (Arrows and CVOX+Arrows)
- **Table:** not announced.

- **Image:** reads alt text "Ryerson Chang School" both Arrow and CVOX + Arrow
- **Form:** focusable, not announced (using Tab key), Arrow keys announces "Combobox. Opt 3, 3 of 3."

Suggested Reading:

- WAI-ARIA Presentation Role
- PowerMapper: Screen Reader Compatibility (Updated Dec 2017)
- Mozilla: ARIA Test Cases

Live Regions

Live regions are used to present changes in web content that occur after a web page has loaded. Typical uses include presenting news feeds, feedback and error messages, or live chat output to screen readers, which would otherwise not know about this content changing or being added to a web page already rendered. Live regions can also be used to announce feedback and error messages when a page loads, so screen reader users do not need to search through a web page to find feedback. It reads automatically when a page finishes loading.

Types of Live Regions

A typical live region can be created by adding aria-live="polite" to any element in which content is updated after a web page has loaded. The "polite" value indicates the priority of the content being updated. In this case, a screen reader will wait for a break in its audio output before announcing the change that occurred. You may also use aria-live="assertive" to interrupt whatever the screen reader is reading, and instead read the changed content before continuing. Typically, "assertive" should be avoided. Only use it in cases where critical information is being updated, such as an error message or critical feedback.

Normally, aria-live would not be used to present feedback or error messages, though it is possible. Instead role="alert", introduced earlier, would be used. Using role="alert" creates an assertive live region that interrupts a screen reader to present its content. They can be used within rendered content to present messages without reloading the page, or they can be used after a page loads, to present the message before any of the other content on the page is read.

In addition to the commonly used role="alert", there are other less commonly used roles that also act as live regions. These are:

- role="log"
- role="marquee"
- role="timer"

- role="status"

Here is the full list of live region attributes:

- aria-live: polite, assertive, off
- aria-relevant: additions, removals, text, all
- aria-atomic: true, false
- aria-busy: true, false
- role="alert"
- role="log"
- role="marquee"
- role="timer"
- role="status"

Suggested Reading: More details on these other Live Region Roles can be found in the WAI-ARIA 1.1 specification.

Care When Using Live Regions

There are a few cases where using a live region (aria-live) to read changing content can create a barrier. Take, for instance, a carousel that presents a series of panels that rotate at a particular frequency. It can be helpful to set up a carousel as a live region, so as each panel slides into view, a screen reader reads the content. However, this behaviour could present a barrier, interfering with the screen reader when it is focused elsewhere, reading other content on the page. If a live region is used with a carousel, it should only be active when the carousel has focus. While typically a live region is created as a static WAI-ARIA attribute, in this case, it should be dynamically added on focus and dynamically removed on blur.

For carousels, it is also important to consider the rate at which panels rotate, ensuring that screen readers have enough time to read the content of the panel before rotating on to the next. This timing can be difficult to predict. It depends on the amount of content on each panel, which can vary significantly, and the rate at which users have their reading rate set on their screen reader. One solution to this issue may be to make the carousel manually rotate when it has focus so users can proceed to the next panel only when they are ready.

Another case where live regions can be problematic is with timers. Timers counting by seconds can essentially render the rest of the content on a page unusable for a screen reader user. As the screen reader announces every second, it interrupts the reading of the other content on a page. Timers that increment each minute, for instance, would not have this problem.

Other places where live regions may be problematic are with very active news or Twitter feeds. Though live regions can be useful for this type of updating content, if there is a constant stream of updates or updates occur frequently, screen reader users may have difficulty comprehending other page content with the frequent interruptions.

Try This: To experience the aggravation of a constantly updating live region, open ChromeVox and give focus to the timer below. In this case, the timer is in an iframe, so you can simply set focus outside the iframe to stop it from reading. If the timer were embedded in the content of the page itself, you would not have this option, and the rest of the page would become unusable with a screen reader. The only option would be to leave the page.

Key Point: Be aware of potential barriers that can be created when live regions are used with high-frequency content updates.

Activity 4: WAI-ARIA Landmarks and Alerts

WAI-ARIA Landmarks and Alerts

Landmarks were added to the WAI-ARIA specification as a way of providing easy navigation within a web page for assistive technology users. Prior to landmarks, bypass links were often used (and still are) that would allow a screen reader user to jump from the top of a page, typically, to an anchor strategically placed further down the page. In the first part of this activity you will add a set of landmark roles to a website user interface (UI).

Live regions were introduced in WAI-ARIA as a way to present changing content to assistive technology users. Feedback messages are good candidates for a live region, so the content of a feedback message is read to the user automatically when it appears without the need to search the page to determine whether an action completed successfully or, alternately, if an action produced an error message. The WAI-ARIA "alert" role is a type of live region ideal for presenting error or success feedback messages. In Part 2 of this activity, you'll add role="alert" to the error messages when the form in the landmarks.html file is submitted with missing or invalid required fields, and when it is submitted successfully.

In your copy of the activity files, open and edit the landmarks.html file. When you have completed both parts of the activity, commit the file back to your GitHub Pages repository, or upload it to the location you have chosen to post your activity files for marking or submit a GitHack URL.

Requirements

Part 1: Landmarks

Add the appropriate landmark roles to elements within the page. Be sure all content within the page is contained within a landmarked region and, depending on the type of content on the page, apply the correct landmark for that type of content.

When you have added all the appropriate landmarks, test the file with ChromeVox (keys: Cvox + L + semicolon) to be sure they are all functioning properly.

Part 2: Live Error and Feedback Messages

The form on the page has three required fields. If you submit the form without valid input for these fields, an error message is generated below each field that has invalid input. Add role="alert" to the first error message, so, when it appears, it is automatically read by ChromeVox along with sending focus to the first field in error so it can be corrected. Do the same for the feedback message that appears when the form is submitted without errors.

HINT: look in join.lib.js in the activity files.

Grading Rubric

Criteria	Points
Content Contained: All content is contained within a landmarked region.	2.0 pts
Correct Landmarks: Appropriate landmarks have been used for each region.	3.0 pts
Messages Announced: The first Error/Feedback message is announced when the form is submitted with and without invalid input. When the first required field is corrected, the next Error/Feedback message is announced, and so on, so any field with invalid content is read aloud.	4.0 pts
Landmarks Distinguishable: Landmark regions with the same role are distinguishable from each other.	1.0 pts
Total Points:	10.0

Self-Test 3

Answer the following questions to test your understanding of key lessons in this unit. This quiz is not being marked.

4

Interactive WAI-ARIA (Basic)

Toggle Buttons (Activity Example)

The remainder of the instruction here is hands-on. You'll be taking inaccessible widgets, like the example of toggle buttons described here, and making them accessible by adding appropriate WAI-ARIA and keyboard operability. The toggle buttons widget demonstrated here is provided as an example for the ten widgets you will be working on over the next three units, describing the Activity Elements you will find in each exercise.

Activity Element: Following the short introduction to the widget above, a list of the WAI-ARIA roles, states, and properties used with the widget are listed.

Roles, states, and properties for toggle buttons

- role="button"
- tabindex="0"
- aria-label="[button name]"
- aria-pressed="[true|false]"

Activity Element: Where available, a Suggested Reading is included that provides additional information about accessibility features for the widget being discussed, often linking to the W3C WAI-ARIA 1.1 Authoring Practice documentation, or to a similar resource. These readings are optional but recommended.

Suggested Reading: Read more about buttons in the WAI-ARIA 1.1 Authoring Practices.

Activity Element: Each widget will have an inaccessible JSFiddle version provided, like the one below. You can examine the JavaScript and HTML to observe how the widget was created. Under the Result tab, view and try out the widget to see how it functions. CSS is also provided, though you will not be working with CSS as part of the activities. In the JSFiddle here, the accessibility elements are included but commented out so you can see how the code snippets below have been applied. In the activities that follow, the accessibility elements will not be present. Your task will be to apply the code snippets yourself to make the inaccessible version provided in the activity file accessible.

At the top right, you may choose to "Edit in JSFiddle" and test the code snippets that will be provided below, to understand how they add accessibility to the widget. You can start by uncommenting the accessibility elements for the toggle buttons, and testing the resulting version with ChromeVox.

The following JSFiddle presents a typical toggle button. Review the JavaScript and HTML markup. Test the buttons present under the Result tab with ChromeVox to understand how it functions without any accessibility features added (if it functions at all). You can work in JSFiddle itself by clicking "Edit in JSFiddle" and copying the accessibility/WAI-ARIA code described below to fix the accessibility of the toggle buttons, before completing the Activity on the page that follows (there is no activity that follows in this example case).

Key Point: The code that appears under the JavaScript tab is not exactly as it appears in the activity files. The $(document.ready{}) function at the top is copied from the associated HTML file for the widget, and the contents of ik_util.js have been appended, so the widget will function in JSFiddle. You will not need to include these in the JavaScript file from the activity files that you will be editing for each widget.

Activity Element: Following the JSFiddle will be a collection of code snippets hosted in PasteBin. These code snippets can be applied to the code presented in the JSFiddle and applied to the code in the activity files, which you will be submitting for marking.

Add a tabindex to each button to make them keyboard focusable, define the role="button", and add a label with aria-label="[button name]" and set the default state to "not pressed" with aria-pressed="false".

Add in equivalent keyboard access where mouse access is provided, referencing the onActivate() function, described below, with jQuery .on('keydown').

Set aria-pressed="[true|false]" for buttons when activated or deactivated to announce the button's state to screen readers.

Adding Keyboard Operability

Keyboard access for the buttons is fairly simple, with no special key press events needing to be defined.

Activity Element: When the WAI-ARIA 1.1 Authoring Practices has a set of recommended keyboard interactions, they will be reproduced here. Widgets will typically follow the recommended practice, though in some cases keyboard interaction may vary.

Keyboard Interaction for Toggle Buttons

When the button has focus:

- ❖ Space: Activates the button.
- ❖ Enter: Activates the button.
- ❖ Following button activation, focus is set depending on the type of action the button performs. For example:
- ❖ If activating the button opens a dialog, the focus moves inside the dialog (see dialog pattern).
- ❖ If activating the button closes a dialog, focus typically returns to the button that opened the dialog unless the function performed in the dialog context logically leads to a different element. For example, activating a cancel button in a dialog returns focus to the button that opened the dialog. However, if the dialog were confirming the action of deleting the page from which it was opened, the focus would logically move to a new context.
- ❖ If activating the button does not dismiss the current context, then focus typically remains on the button after activation, e.g., an Apply or Recalculate button.
- ❖ If the button action indicates a context change, such as move to next step in a wizard or add another search criteria, then it is often appropriate to move focus to the starting point for that action.
- ❖ If the button is activated with a shortcut key, the focus usually remains in the context from which the shortcut key was activated. For example, if Alt + U were assigned to an "Up" button that moves the currently focused item in a list one position higher in the list, pressing Alt + U when the focus is in the list would not move the focus from the list.

Source: W3C WAI-ARIA 1.1 Authoring Practices

Activity Element: Though this widget requires no keyboard interaction beyond that provided in ik_utils.js to handle space bar and Enter keys, other widgets will have a custom function provided here that defines possible keyboard interactions for those widgets. In most cases, that code can be copied as is into the widget's JavaScript file.

No added keyboard interaction is required for the toggle buttons beyond the standard Space bar and Enter key defined in the ik_utils.js file. Reference to these key events is added to the onActivate() function.

Accessible Toggle Buttons in Action

Activity Element: Each widget will have a short video of it interacting with ChromeVox. When completing the activities, aim to have your activity submission function as presented in the video.

The buttons are accessed initially with the Tab key, and the Tab key is used to move between buttons. The Space bar or Enter keys are used to activate and deactivate buttons. Aim to have the widget you edit in the associated activity function like that presented in the video (there is no associated activity for this example).

Video: Accessible Toggle Buttons

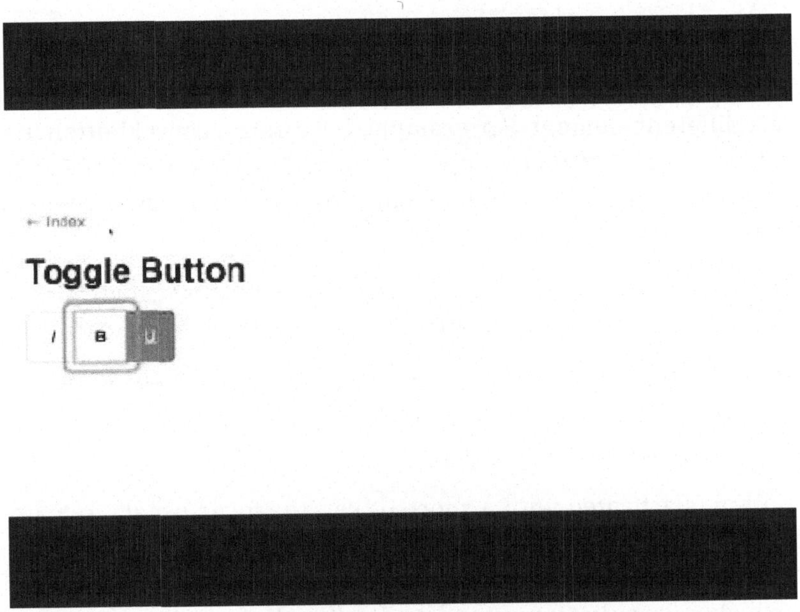

A YouTube element has been excluded from this version of the text. You can view it online here: https://pressbooks.library.ryerson.ca/wafd/?p=324

Suggestion Boxes

A suggestion box (aka, combo box or autocomplete box) is a type of selection menu that helps users enter a correct choice. They are typically made up of a text entry field and a list of choices based on a number of characters entered into the text field. In the example provided here, entering a few characters brings up a list of countries that contain those characters.

Because the text entry field is a standard form text input field, it will be accessible by default. No additional coding is required to make it accessible. What needs the most attention is the list of choices, which needs to announce itself when it appears and needs to be keyboard navigable.

WAI-ARIA roles, states, and properties used in a suggestion box

- role='region'
- aria-live='polite'
- aria-describedby='[id of instructions div]'

Suggested Reading: For details on constructing accessible suggestion boxes, refer to: WAI-ARIA Best Practices: Combo Box.

The following JSFiddle presents a typical suggestion box. Review the JavaScript and HTML markup, and test the suggestion box presented under the Result tab with ChromeVox to understand how it functions without any accessibility features added. You can work in JSFiddle itself by clicking "Edit in JSFiddle", copying the accessibility/ WAI-ARIA code described below to fix the accessibility of the suggestion box, before completing Activity 5, on the page that follows.

Define some instructions to make it clear there will be suggestions appearing when text is entered into the text input field.

When the suggestion box receives focus, generate the instructions for it by adding the notify() function to the onFocus() function to produce a live region with the instruction text. This instruction text is then read automatically when a screen reader encounters the

Within the init() function, create a <div> to use as a live region, adding aria-live="polite" to announce the list usage instructions defined above when the text field receives focus. Also, give it a role="region" so it can be found in the landmarks list.

Provide additional instructions when the suggestion box is populated, adding to the getSuggestions() function.

Adding Keyboard Operability

WAI-ARIA best practices defines all recommended suggestion box keyboard functionality, listed below. In our example, only the required keyboard events are included.

Suggestion Box Keyboard Interaction

When focus is in the textbox:

- ❖ Down Arrow: If the popup is available, moves focus into the popup:
- ❖ If the autocomplete behaviour automatically selected a suggestion before Down Arrow was pressed, focus is placed on the suggestion following the automatically selected suggestion.
- ❖ Otherwise, places focus on the first focusable element in the popup.
- ❖ Up Arrow (Optional): If the popup is available, places focus on the last focusable element in the popup.
- ❖ Esc: Dismisses the popup if it is visible. Optionally, clears the textbox.
- ❖ Enter: If an autocomplete suggestion is automatically selected, accepts the suggestion either by placing the input cursor at the end of the accepted value in the textbox or by performing a default action on the value. For example, in a messaging application, the default action may be to add the accepted value to a list of message recipients and then clear the textbox so the user can add another recipient.
- ❖ Printable Characters: Type characters in the textbox. Note that some implementations may regard certain characters as invalid and prevent their input.
- ❖ Standard single line text editing keys appropriate for the device platform (see note below).
- ❖ Alt+Down Arrow (Optional): If the popup is available but not displayed, displays the popup without moving focus.
- ❖ Alt+Up Arrow (Optional): If the popup is displayed:
- ❖ If the popup contains focus, returns focus to the textbox.
- ❖ the popup.

Note: Standard single line text editing keys appropriate for the device platform:

- ❖ include keys for input, cursor movement, selection, and text manipulation.
- ❖ Standard key assignments for editing functions depend on the device operating system.
- ❖ The most robust approach for providing text editing functions is to rely on browsers, which supply them for HTML inputs with type text and for elements with the contenteditable HTML attribute.

- ❖ IMPORTANT: Be sure that JavaScript does not interfere with browser-provided text editing functions by capturing key events for the keys used to perform them.

  Source: W3C WAI-ARIA 1.1 Best Practices

The most significant effort in making the suggestion box accessible is adding keyboard operability. In our case, we'll add Up and Down Arrow operability to the list box. Create a switch that captures the keypress event. If it's a Down Arrow, select the next item down in the list. If it's an Up Arrow, select the previous item. If it's any character key, enter the value in the text field. Add this to the onKeyUp() function, while integrating the existing functionality in the function into the default for the switch statement.

Accessible Suggestion Box in Action

Watch the following video to see how ChromeVox interacts with a suggestion box. When the suggestion box receives focus, instructions are read. When the second letter is typed into the text field a list of suggestions appears below. Additional instructions are provided on how to make a selection from the list. Arrow keys are used to navigate through the suggestions, and the Enter key is used to select one of them. Aim to have the suggestion box you update in Activity 5 on the following page operate and announce like the one in the video.

Video: Accessible Suggest Box

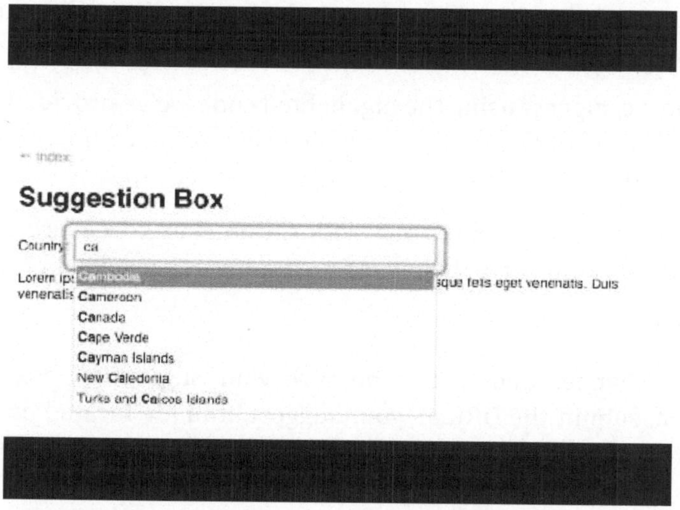

A YouTube element has been excluded from this version of the text. You can view it online here: https://pressbooks.library.ryerson.ca/wafd/?p=330

Activity 5: Accessible Suggestion Box

Accessible Suggestion Box

Based on the Suggestion Box details on the previous page, apply what you have learned to the associated activity files to make the suggestion box provided accessible.

Files for this activity include:

- /suggest.html
- /assets/ik_suggest.js

Use the surroundings of the highlighted code on the previous page as a guide to find where the fixes should be applied. Repair the accessibility of the suggestion box by applying the highlighted code to the /assets/ik_suggest.js file.

Note: While we suggest using the highlighted code we've provided, you are free to come up with your own solutions provided they produce the expected results listed in the marking rubric below.

Test your updated suggestion box with ChromeVox to ensure each element described in the marking rubric below is functioning as suggested.

Requirements

Apply your changes and test to be sure your suggestion box functions as described. Then, submit the URL of your suggest.html file located on your GitHub site, on the web server you are using to host your copy of the activity files, or a GitHack URL.

Grading Rubric

Criteria	Points
Initial Instructions: Instructions are provided when the country field receives focus.	2.0 pts
Announce Suggestions Present: The suggestion list is announced when suggestions are available.	2.0 pts
Suggestion Instructions Instructions are provided when suggestions are available.	1.0 pts
Keyboard Access: A country selection can be made using only the keyboard	5.0 pts
Total Points:	10.0

Tooltips

A tooltip is typically used to display some information about its owning element when a user hovers a mouse pointer over or gives keyboard focus to an element. Tooltips might include a definition for a word, perhaps full wording for an acronym or abbreviation, or maybe instructions on how to operate a tool or widget. There are many possibilities.

Tooltips are an enhancement for the default "title text" standard with HTML. They provide much more flexibility in the presentation and types of information that can be presented than a standard title text tooltip.

WAI-ARIA roles, states, and properties used in a tooltip

- role="tooltip"
- aria-hidden:[true|false]
- aria-live="polite"
- tabindex = [0|-1]

Suggested Reading: For details on constructing accessible tooltips, refer to: WAI-ARIA Best Practices: Tooltips.

The following JSFiddle presents a typical tooltip. Review the JavaScript and HTML markup. Test the tooltip presented under the Result tab with ChromeVox to understand how it functions without any accessibility features added. You can work in JSFiddle by clicking "Edit in JSFiddle", copying the accessibility/WAI-ARIA code described below to fix the accessibility of the tooltip before completing Activity 6 on the page that follows.

The first thing to add to the init() function, where the tooltip <span> element is defined, are the WAI-ARIA attributes. First, define the tooltip with role="tooltip". Hide the tooltip by default with aria-hidden="true". Also, add a live region with aria-live="polite", so screen readers automatically read the tooltip when it appears. Note, the WAI-ARIA 1.1 best practices recommend using aria-describedby within the owning element to reference the content of a tooltip, which does not announce as expected with current versions of Chrome. Instead, we use aria-live, which announces correctly across all current browsers.

Next, add keyboard focus to the element the tooltip belongs to with tabindex="0", and add focus to .on('mouseover'), so both a mouse hover and keyboard focus open the tooltip.

Also, further down in the owning element's definition, add aria-hidden="false" so the hidden-by-default tooltip becomes visible when the mouse hover or keyboard focus occurs.

Also, added here is aria-hidden="true" to be sure the tooltip is hidden from screen readers, should a mouseout event close the tooltip, adding it to . on(mouseout) chained to the element ($elem) definition.

Adding Keyboard Operability

WAI-ARIA best practices defines keyboard interaction for a tooltip as follows:

Recommended Keyboard Interaction for a Tooltip

Tooltip widgets do not receive focus. A hover that contains focusable elements can be made using a non-modal dialog.

- Esc: Dismisses the Tooltip.

Note:

- Focus stays on the triggering element while the tooltip is displayed.
- If the tooltip is invoked when the trigger element receives focus, then it is dismissed when it no longer has focus (onBlur). If the tooltip is invoked with mouseIn, then it is dismissed with mouseOut.

Source: W3C WAI-ARIA Best Practices 1.1

Keyboard operability for a tooltip or, rather, the owning element is relatively simple. As a keyboard equivalent for the .on(mouseout) described above, . on(blur) is chained to the $elem element and within it aria-hidden="true" hides the tooltip again, if the mouse pointer is not over the element.

Also, if the Esc key is used, add aria-hidden="true" to hide the tooltip, even if the mouse is hovering, or the owning element has focus.

Accessible Tooltip in Action

Watch the following video to see how ChromeVox interacts with a tooltip. The Tab key is used to navigate to the first tooltip, which opens a live region when its content is read aloud. Pressing the Tab key once again, move focus to the text input field, and a second tooltip opens and its content is read aloud. Aim to have the tooltips you update in Activity 6 on the following page operate and announce like the one in the video.

Video: Accessible Tooltips

A YouTube element has been excluded from this version of the text. You can view it online here: https://pressbooks.library.ryerson.ca/wafd/?p=336

Activity 6: Accessible Tooltips

Accessible Tooltips

Based on the Tooltip details on the previous page, apply what you have learned to the associated activity files to make the tooltips there accessible.

Files for this activity include:

- /tooltip.html
- /assets/ik_tooltip.js

Use the surroundings of the highlighted code on the previous page as a guide to find where the fixes should be applied. Repair the accessibility of the tooltips by applying the highlighted code to the /assets/ik_tooltip.js file.

Note: While we suggest using the highlighted code we've provided, you are free to come up with your own solutions provided they produce the expected results listed in the marking rubric below.

Test your updated tooltips with ChromeVox to ensure each element described in the marking rubric below is functioning as suggested.

Requirements

When you have applied your changes and tested to be sure your tooltips function as described, submit the URL to your tooltip.html file on your GitHub Pages site, to the file on the web server you are using to host your copy of the activity files, or to a Githack URL.

Grading Rubric

Criteria	Points
Tooltips Open: Tooltips open when their owning element receives keyboard focus or mouseover.	3.0 pts
Tooltips Read: Tooltips read aloud when their owning element receives keyboard focus or mouseover.	3.0 pts
Tooltips Hides: Tooltips hide when focus is removed or on mouseout.	2.0 pts
Tooltips Escape: Tooltips hide when the Esc key is pressed.	2.0 pts
Total Points:	10.0

Progress Bars

Progress bars are typically implemented when a user has to wait for a process to complete, whether that may be waiting for an upload to finish, data to be compiled, a report to be generated, or any other process that takes more than a few seconds to complete.

For most users, there is generally a visual representation of progress, such as a status bar or a circular progress indicator. As a process progresses, a viewer can estimate when it will be complete. For blind users, however, the visual presentation provides no useful information, so they will need to be able to retrieve the current value some other way.

Roles, states, and properties in a progress bar

- role="progressbar"
- tabindex = [0|-1]
- aria-valuenow = "0"
- aria-valuemin = "0"
- aria-valuemax = "[max value define in default options]"
- aria-describedby = "[instruction ID]"
- role = "region"
- aria-live = "assertive"
- aria-atomic = "additions"
- aria-hidden = "[true|false]"

Suggested Reading: For more about accessible progress bars, see WAI-ARIA 1.1: Progressbar

The following JSFiddle presents a typical progress bar widget. Review the JavaScript and HTML markup and test the progress bar presented under the result tab with ChromeVox to understand how it functions without any accessibility features added. You can work in JSFiddle itself by clicking the Edit in "JSFiddle" at the top, right-hand side. Copy the accessibility/WAI-ARIA code described below to fix the accessibility of the progress bar before completing Activity 7 on the page that follows.

WAI-ARIA to Make the Progress Bar Accessible

Key Point: For the exercise in Activity 7: Accessible Progress Bar, aim to have the progress bar function in ChromeVox, but, be aware that solutions described here will not work in other screen readers.

In this example, we have added WAI-ARIA to a progress bar, but due to limited support for the WAI-ARIA progressbar attributes by screen readers other than ChromeVox, there is also a workaround using the jQuery .data() function to output the current value for users of JAWS or NVDA screen readers. You can refer to the ik_progressbar_data.js file for the workaround. However, for Activity 7, be sure to start from the ik_progressbar.js file for the assignment submission. To experiment with the .data() version of the progress bar JavaScript file, you can adjust the reference to the file in the progressbar.html file.

First, as is typical, create some instructions describing how to operate the progress bar with a screen reader and keyboard and add them to the default options.

Update the init() function to add the required WAI-ARIA. First set tabindex="-1" to be sure the bar itself is not keyboard focusable by default, and associate the bar with the instructions so when the bar does receive focus the instructions are read. Set some default values for aria-valuemin, aria-valuenow, and aria-valuemax. Also, add keyboard access to the bar with an on(keydown) reference to the onKeyDown() function, described below.

Add to the notifications <div> live region attributes so when Space/Enter are pressed and the progress percent is added, or if "Loading Complete!" is added, they are read aloud by the screen reader.

Finally, create the <div> with instructions referenced by its ID with aria-describedby added to the bar <div> and hide it by default.

Replace the data(value) in the getValue() function, used to retrieve the current value of the progress bar when the Space bar or Enter keys are pressed, with an aria-valuenow attribute. This replaces the .data(value) needed to function with screen readers other than ChromeVox.

In the setValue() function, add in a tabindex="-1" to remove keyboard focus from the bar when the max value is reached and to add the "Loading Complete" message to the notification <div>. Finally, add either the current value of the progress on keypress or the max value (if progress is complete) to an aria-valuenow attribute. This replaces the .data() work-around, which is needed to function with screen readers other than ChromeVox.

Adding Keyboard Operability

Keyboard access for a progress bar is relatively simple. There is typically no mouse or keyboard interaction. One generally waits and, when progress is complete, continues on with some other action. For screen reader users, however, they will need to be able to get the current progress value using a keypress.

To allow the current value to be retrieved, set up the Enter and Space bar keyboard controls with the onKeyDown() function. This also triggers the notify() function. When one of those keys is pressed, it outputs the value to the notification <div> that we have set up as a live region.

Accessible Progress Bar in Action

Watch the following video to see how ChromeVox interacts with a progress bar. When the Run Demo button is pressed, instructions are provided on how to announce progress. Pressing the Space bar or Enter key announces the percentage progress at any given moment. When progress has finished, "Loading Complete" is announced. Aim to have the progress bar you update in the activity on the following page operate and announce like the one in the video.

Video: Accessible Progress Bar

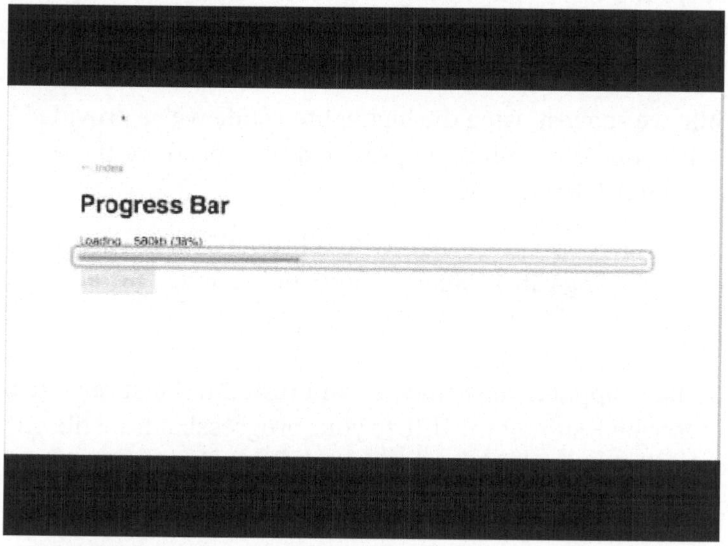

A YouTube element has been excluded from this version of the text. You can view it online here: https://pressbooks.library.ryerson.ca/wafd/?p=341

Activity 7: Accessible Progress Bar

Accessible Progress Bar

Based on the Progress Bar details on the previous page, apply what you have learned to the associated activity files to make the progress bar there accessible.

Files for this activity include:

- /progressbar.html
- /assets/ik_progressbar.js

Use the surroundings of the highlighted code on the previous page as a guide to find where the fixes should be applied. Repair the accessibility of the progress bar by applying the highlighted code to the /assets/ik_progressbar.js file.

Note: While we suggest using the highlighted code we've provided, you are free to come up with your own solutions provided they produce the expected results listed in the marking rubric below.

Test your updated progress bar with ChromeVox to ensure each element described in the marking rubric below is functioning as suggested.

Requirements

When you have applied your changes and tested to be sure your progress bar functions as described, submit the URL to your progressbar.html file on your GitHub Pages site, to the file on the web server you are using to host your copy of the activity files, or to a GitHack URL.

Grading Rubric

Criteria	Points
Instructions Provided: When the progress bar begins running, instructions are provided on how to announce progress percentage.	2.0 pts
Keyboard Announce Progress: The keyboard can be used to announce progress percentage.	5.0 pts
Announce Complete: When progress finishes, Loading Complete is announced.	3.0 pts
Total Points:	10.0

5

Interactive WAI-ARIA (Intermediate)

Sliders

Sliders typically allow users to select a value between minimum and maximum values by dragging a slider thumb along a slider bar or track.

WAI-ARIA roles, states, and properties used in a slider

- tabindex="[0 | -1]"
- role="slider"
- aria-valuemin="[number]"
- aria-valuemax="[number]"
- aria-valuenow="[number]"

Suggested Reading: Additional information about creating accessible sliders can be found in the WAI-ARIA Best Practices.

The following JSFiddle presents a typical slider widget. Review the JavaScript and HTML markup. Test the slider presented under the Result tab with ChromeVox to understand how it functions without any accessibility features added. You can work in JSFiddle itself by clicking the "Edit in JSFiddle" at the top, right-hand side, copying the accessibility/WAI-ARIA code described below to fix the accessibility of the slider before completing Activity 8 on the page that follows.

Define some instructions that describe how to use the slider for screen reader users.

Add a tabindex="0" to make the slider thumb keyboard focusable. Assign a role="slider" to the text box so it announces as a slider instead of a text entry field. Set aria-valuemin, aria-valuemax, and aria-valuenow values, and reference the instructions with aria-describedby. Using .on('keydown') reference the onKeyDown function to add keyboard operability to the slider.

Create a <div> for the screen reader instructions.

Dynamically set the value of aria-valuenow based on the value at which the slider thumb is located.

Remove keyboard access from the original text field.

Adding Keyboard Operability

WAI-ARIA authoring practices defines recommended keyboard functionality for a slider, listed below.

Keyboard Interaction for a Slider

- Right Arrow: Increase the value of the slider by one step.
- Up Arrow: Increase the value of the slider by one step.
- Left Arrow: Decrease the value of the slider by one step.
- Down Arrow: Decrease the value of the slider by one step.
- Home: Set the slider to the first allowed value in its range.
- End: Set the slider to the last allowed value in its range.
- Page Up (Optional): Increment the slider by an amount larger than the step change made by Up Arrow.
- Page Down (Optional): Decrement the slider by an amount larger than the step change made by Down Arrow.

Note:

- Focus is placed on the slider (the visual object that the mouse user would move, also known as the thumb).
- In some circumstances, reversing the direction of the value change for the keys specified above (e.g., having Up Arrow decrease the value) could create a more intuitive experience.

Source: W3C WAI-ARIA 1.1 Best Practices

Add keyboard event handling to our slider widget. In our case, we will add Left and Right Arrow controls for moving the slider thumb along the slider bar, and End and Home controls for moving the slider thumb between the start and end of the slider bar.

Accessible Slider in Action

Watch the following video of ChromeVox interacting with a slider. The Arrow keys are used to move the slider thumb along the slider bar, and the Home and End keys are used to move the slider thumb between the start and the end of the slider bar. You may notice that ChromeVox interprets "min" as "minute" rather than min and max that define the range along the slider bar. Aim to have the slider you update in the activity that follows on the next page operate and announce like the one in the video.

Video: Accessible Slider

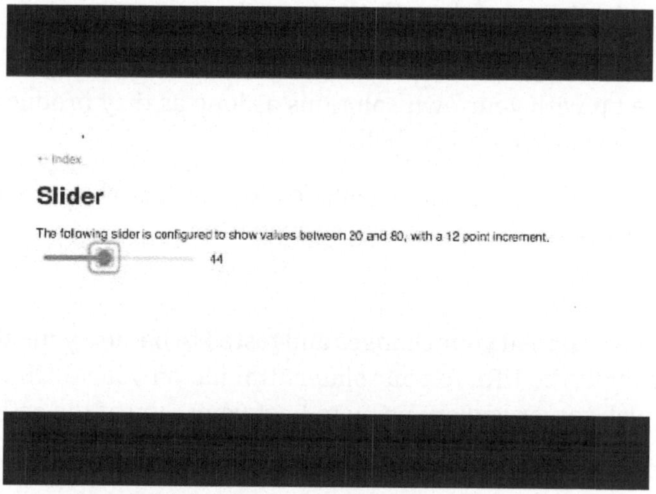

A YouTube element has been excluded from this version of the text. You can view it online here: https://pressbooks.library.ryerson.ca/wafd/?p=349

Activity 8: Accessible Slider

Accessible Slider

Based on the Slider details on the previous page, apply what you have learned to the associated activity files to make the slider there accessible.

Files for this activity include:

- /slider.html
- /assets/ik_slider.js

Use the code surrounding the highlighted solutions on the previous page as a guide to find where the fixes should be applied. Repair the accessibility of the slider by applying the highlighted code to the /assets/ik_slider.js file.

Note: While we suggest using the highlighted solutions we've provided, you are free to come up with your own solutions as long as they produce the expected results listed in the marking rubric below.

Test your updated slider with ChromeVox to ensure each element described in the marking rubric below is functioning as suggested.

Requirements

When you have applied your changes and tested to be sure your slider functions as described, submit the URL to your slider.html file on your GitHub Pages site, to the file on the web server you are using to host your copy of the activity files, or to a GitHack URL.

Grading Rubric

Criteria	Points
Slider Focusable: Slider thumb is keyboard focusable.	2.0 pts
Keyboard Operable: Slider thumb moves using Left and Right Arrow keys, and the Home and End keys.	5.0 pts
Min/Max Values Announced: Minimum and maximum values are announced.	1.0 pts
Value Announced: When the slider moves, its new value is announced.	2.0 pts
Total Points:	10.0

Accordions

Accordion widgets can come in single or multi-select formats, in which one or multiple panels can be opened at once, respectively. They are typically used to reduce the space that content occupies and to reduce scrolling. Accordions are made up of Accordion Headers and Accordion Panels. The accordion headers control the display of their associated accordion panel.

The WAI-ARIA roles, states, and properties used in an accordion

- aria-multiselectable ="(true | false)"
- role="heading"
- role="button"
- aria-controls="[panel id]"
- tabindex="0"
- role="region"
- aria-hidden= "(true | false)"
- aria-expanded= "(true | false)"

Suggested Reading: For details on constructing accessible accordions, refer to: WAI-ARIA Authoring Practices: Accordion

The following JSFiddle presents a typical accordion widget. Review the JavaScript and HTML markup. Test the accordion presented under the Result tab with ChromeVox to understand how it functions without any accessibility features added. You can work in JSFiddle itself by clicking "Edit in JSFiddle", copying the accessibility/WAI-ARIA code described below to fix the accessibility of the accordion before completing Activity 9 on the page that follows.

First, add the accordion to the landmarked regions by assigning role="region" to the opening <DL> element when the accordion is initialized, adding the region role to the init() function.

Next, add the aria-multiselectable attribute to the <DL>, which will be dynamically set to true or false based on plugin configuration settings. This lets a user know that more than one accordion panel can be opened when set to TRUE or only a single panel when set to FALSE. Refer to the $(document).ready block in the HTML, where the assignment takes place.

The semantics of the children of the <DL> element, which was assigned role="presentation", will also have their definition list semantics removed. Add the accordion semantics role="heading" to assign a heading role to the <DT> elements. The aria-level attribute might be used to implement nested accordion panels, but for our purpose here a simplified version is sufficient.

Add a <div> inside the header (i.e., DT) and define its role as a button. The button is given an aria-controls attribute to define which of the accordion panels it controls.

By default the toggle state is set to false with aria-expanded="false" to be updated dynamically when the button is clicked or key pressed. Finally add tabindex="0" to the button (<div>) to make it keyboard focusable.

The tabindex will make the button focusable, but it will not make it clickable. The .on() jQuery function adds a click event to the button, but a keypress event must also be added. Adding .on('keydown') activates the onKeyDown function, defined below, so the accordion headers operate with both a mouse click and a keypress.

In the togglePanel() function, before autoCollapse(), add in the toggle to add and update the aria-expanded attribute for the panel headers, based on whether the associated panel is visible or not.

Within the autoCollapse() function, toggle aria-expanded="false" and aria-hidden="true" for all accordion tabs that are not the current one. This ensures only one panel is open at a time.

Finally, the accordion panel semantics are added, defining the <DD> elements that had its semantics removed when role="presentation" was added to the parent <DL>. Panels are given a generic role="region" to make the panel browsable in the landmarks list, set to be hidden by default with aria-hidden="true" so all panels are closed when the page loads. Further, tabindex="0" is also added to make the panels keyboard focusable so the content of the panel is read as the user navigates to them.

Adding Keyboard Operability

WAI-ARIA best practices defines all recommended accordion keyboard functionality, listed below. In our example, only the required keyboard events are included.

Keyboard Interaction for Accordions

- Enter or Space:
- When focus is on the accordion header for a collapsed panel, expands the associated panel. If the implementation allows only one panel to be expanded, and if another panel is expanded, collapses that panel.
- When focus is on the accordion header for an expanded panel, collapses the panel if the implementation supports collapsing. Some implementations require one panel to be expanded at all times and allow only one panel to be expanded; so they do not support a collapse function.
- Down Arrow (Optional): If focus is on an accordion header, moves focus to the next accordion header. If focus is on the last accordion header, either does nothing or moves focus to the first accordion header.

- Up Arrow (Optional): If focus is on an accordion header, moves focus to the previous accordion header. If focus is on the first accordion header, either does nothing or moves focus to the last accordion header.
- Home (Optional): When focus is on an accordion header, moves focus to the first accordion header.
- End (Optional): When focus is on an accordion header, moves focus to the last accordion header.
- Ctrl+Page Down (Optional): If focus is inside an accordion panel or on an accordion header, moves focus to the next accordion header. If focus is in the last accordion header or panel, either does nothing or moves focus to the first accordion header.
- Ctrl+Page Up (Optional): If focus is inside an accordion panel, moves focus to the header for that panel. If focus is on an accordion header, moves focus to the previous accordion header. If focus is on the first accordion header, either does nothing or moves focus to the last accordion header.

  Source: WAI-ARIA Accordion Design Patterns

The following onKeyDown function has been created to add keyboard operability to the header elements of the accordion, allowing both Space bar and Enter keys to operate the toggles (i.e., headers) that open and close panels, and the Arrow keys to move between the accordion headers. By default, users can navigate between headers, and between headers and panels using the Tab key.

Accessible Accordion in Action

Watch the following video to see how ChromeVox interacts with an accordion. The Tab key is used to navigate into the accordions, move between accordion headers, and move between accordion headers and panels. Arrow keys can also be used to move between accordion headers, but not from headers to an associated panel. Aim to have the accordion you update in the activity on the following page operate and announce like the one in the video.

Video: Accessible Accordions

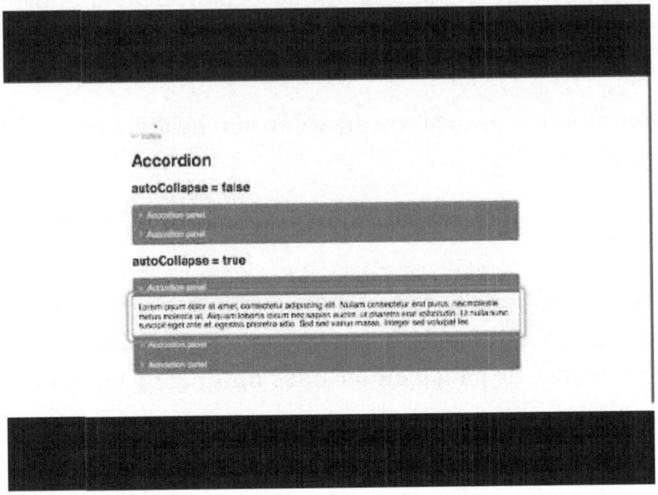

A YouTube element has been excluded from this version of the text. You can view it online here: https://pressbooks.library.ryerson.ca/wafd/?p=353

Activity 9: Accessible Accordion

Accessible Accordion

Based on the Accordion details on the previous page, apply what you have learned to the associated activity files to make the accordion there accessible.

Files for this activity include:

- /accordion.html
- /assets/ik_accordion.js

Use the surroundings of the highlighted code on the previous page as a guide to find where the fixes should be applied. Repair the accessibility of the accordion by applying the highlighted code to the /assets/ik_accordion.js file.

Note: While we suggest using the highlighted code we've provided, you are free to come up with your own solutions provided they produce the expected results listed in the marking rubric below.

Test your updated accordion with ChromeVox to ensure each element described in the marking rubric below is functioning as suggested.

Requirements

When you have applied your changes and tested to be sure your accordion functions as described, submit the URL to your accordion.html file on your GitHub Pages site, to the file on the web server you are using to host your copy of the activity files, or a GitHack URL.

Grading Rubric

Criteria	Points
Header Focus: Accordion headers are keyboard focusable.	1.0 pts
Headers as Buttons: Accordion headers are announced as buttons instead of list items.	2.0 pts
Open Panels: Accordion headers open panels with a click or key press.	2.0 pts
Expand/Collapse: Accordions announce expanded when a panel is opened and collapsed when closed.	2.0 pts
Panels Focusable: Accordion panels are focusable with a Tab key press when opened.	2.0 pts
Header Navigation: Navigation between accordion headers with Up and Down Arrow keys, and the Tab key.	1.0 pts
Total Points:	10.0

Tab Panels

Tab panels, much like accordions, are often used to conserve space and reduce scrolling. They are typically made up of a tablist that contains a series of tabs, each tab controlling the display of a panel. As each tab is activated, its associated panel is displayed and other panels are hidden. When a tab is selected, it is highlighted to indicate which tab and panel are active.

WAI-ARIA roles, states, and properties used in a tab panel

- ❖ role="tablist"
- ❖ role="tabpanel"
- ❖ role="tab"

- aria-hidden="[true|false]"
- tabindex = [0 | -1]
- aria-controls="[panel id]"
- aria-selected="[true|false]"

Suggested Reading: Additional information about creating accessible tab panels can be found in the WAI-ARIA Authoring Practices.

The following JSFiddle presents a typical tab panel widget. Review the JavaScript and HTML markup. Test the tab panel presented under the Result tab with ChromeVox to understand how it functions without any accessibility features added. You can work in JSFiddle itself by clicking "Edit in JSFiddle", copying the accessibility/WAI-ARIA code described below to fix the accessibility of the tab panel before completing Activity 10 on the page that follows.

In our case, we are generating the tabs for each child <div> defined in the HTML, though tabs and tab panels could be static HTML. The tablist is made up of a <ul> and child <li> elements. We assign role="tablist" to the <ul> to remove its list semantics and replace it with tab panel semantics.

Next, we add WAI-ARIA to the panels, assigning role="tabpanel" to each of the original <div> elements, hide them by default with aria-hidden="true", and finally adding tabindex="0" to make the panels keyboard focusable.

The tabs themselves are now defined, replacing the list item semantics with tab semantics adding role="tab" to each of the <li> elements generated. We also need to define which tab controls which tabpanel, dynamically generating aria-controls="[panel_id]" for each of the tabs.

When a tab is selected, we want to remove selection from other tabs with aria-selected="false", and remove keyboard access temporarily by assigning tabindex="-1" to the unselected tabs, so that that tabpanel becomes next in the tab order, and users can navigate directly from the tab to the panel without having to pass through the other tabs in the tablist.

Likewise, when a tab is selected we assign aria-selected="true" so screen readers announce the selected tab, we add tabindex="0" as the roving tabindex to make that tab focusable.

As the tabs change, hide all the panels with aria-hidden="true" so screen readers do not see them, then open the panel the current tab controls with aria-hidden="false" so screen readers can see the active panel. These are added to the end of the selectTab() function.

Adding Keyboard Operability

W3C describes authoring practices for tab panel keyboard interactions as follows.

Keyboard Interaction for Tab Panels

For the tab list:

- **Tab:** When focus moves into the tab list, places focus on the active tab element. When the tab list contains the focus, moves focus to the next element in the page tab sequence outside the tablist, which is typically either the first focusable element inside the tab panel or the tab panel itself.
- When focus is on a tab element in a horizontal tab list:
  - **Left Arrow:** moves focus to the previous tab. If focus is on the first tab, moves focus to the last tab. Optionally, activates the newly focused tab (See note below).
  - **Right Arrow:** Moves focus to the next tab. If focus is on the last tab element, moves focus to the first tab. Optionally, activates the newly focused tab (See note below).
- When focus is on a tab in a tablist with either horizontal or vertical orientation:
  - **Space or Enter:** Activates the tab if it was not activated automatically on focus.
  - **Home (Optional):** Moves focus to the first tab
  - **(Optional):** Moves focus to the last tab.
  - **Shift + F10:** If the tab has an associated pop-up menu, opens the menu.
  - **Delete (Optional):** If deletion is allowed, deletes (closes) the current tab element and its associated tab panel. If any tabs remain, sets focus to the tab following the tab that was closed and activates the newly focused tab. Alternatively, or in addition, the delete function is available in a context menu.

Note:

- It is recommended that tabs activate automatically when they receive focus as long as their associated tab panels are displayed without noticeable latency. This typically requires tab panel content to be preloaded. Otherwise, automatic activation slows focus movement, which significantly hampers users' ability to navigate efficiently across the tab list. For additional guidance, see 5.4 Deciding When to Make Selection Automatically Follow Focus.

- If the tabs in a tab list are arranged vertically:
- Down Arrow performs as Right Arrow is described above.
- Up Arrow performs as Left Arrow is described above.
- If the tab list is horizontal, it does not listen for Down Arrow or Up Arrow so those keys can provide their normal browser scrolling functions even when focus is inside the tab list.

As usual, the tab panel needs to be keyboard operable to be accessible to screen readers. The onKeyDown() function is added to the functions, to add arrow key navigation between tabs, and between tabs and panels. Tab navigation and Enter keys are enabled by default and do not need to be defined here.

The onKeyDown function is then added to each tab, referenced with jQuery's . on('keydown') function, added to the init() function's $tab definition.

Now, with keyboard access and WAI-ARIA added to define the semantics of the tab panel, it should be fully functional for screen readers.

Accessible Tab Panel in Action

Watch the following video showing ChromeVox interacting with a tab panel. The Tab key is used to navigate into the tab panel and to the first tab. The arrow keys are used to move between tabs and, when on a tab, the Tab key is used to navigate to the associated panel. While on a panel, Shift + Tab is used to return to the tablist. There might also be Up and Down arrows enabled to move between tabs and panels, though we have not enabled them here. Aim to have the tab panel you update in the activity coming up on the next page operate and announce itself like the one in the video.

Video: Accessible Tab Panel

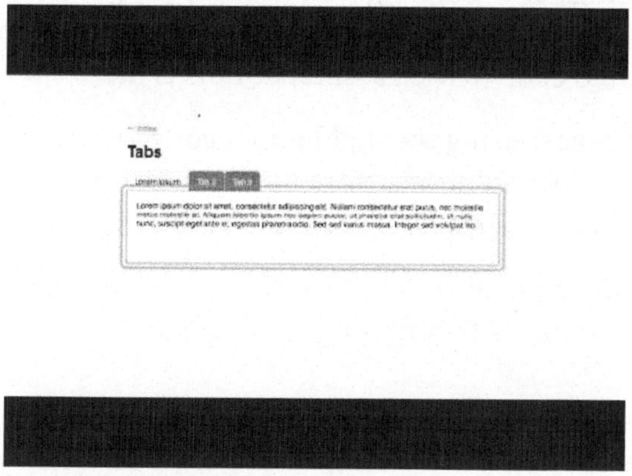

A YouTube element has been excluded from this version of the text. You can view it online here: https://pressbooks.library.ryerson.ca/wafd/?p=357

Activity 10: Accessible Tab Panel

Accessible Tab Panel

Based on the Tab Panel details on the previous page, apply what you have learned to the associated activity files to make the tab panel there accessible.

Files for this activity include:

- /tabs.html
- /assets/ik_tabs.js

Use the surroundings of the highlighted code on the previous page as a guide to find where the fixes should be applied. Repair the accessibility of the tab panel by applying the highlighted code to the /assets/ik_tabs.js file.

Note: While we suggest using the highlighted code we've provided, you are free to come up with your own solutions provided they produce the expected results listed in the marking rubric below.

Test your updated tab panel with ChromeVox to be sure each element described in the marking rubric below is functioning as suggested.

Requirements

When you have applied your changes and tested to ensure your tab panel functions as described, submit the URL to your tabs.html file on your GitHub Pages site, to the file on the web server you are using to host your copy of the activity files, or a GitHack URL.

Grading Rubric

Criteria	Points
List to Tab Semantics: List semantics are replaced with tab panel semantics.	2.0 pts
Tab Position: Focus position in the tablist is announced.	1.0 pts
Tab Focus opens Panel: When a tab is in focus, its associated panel displays.	1.0 pts
Arrow Key Between Tabs: Arrow keys can be used to navigate between tabs.	2.0 pts
Tab Key from Tab to Panel: Tab key can be used to move from a selected tab directly to its associated panel, Shift+Tab to move back to tabs.	2.0 pts
Panels Focusable: Panels are keyboard focusable.	2.0 pts
Total Points:	10.0

Carousels

Carousels are typically used to present a series of panels or images that rotate at a particular frequency.

WAI-ARIA roles, states, and properties used in carousels

- role="region"
- aria-live="polite"
- tabindex="0"

- aria-describedby="[id of div with instructions]"
- aria-hidden="(true|false)"

Suggested Reading: The Carousel Tutorial from the W3C provides additional details on constructing accessible carousels.

The following JSFiddle presents a typical carousel widget. Review the JavaScript and HTML markup. Test the carousel presented under the Result tab with ChromeVox to understand how it functions without any accessibility features added. You can work in JSFiddle itself by clicking "Edit in JSFiddle." Copy the accessibility/ WAI-ARIA code described below to fix the accessibility of the accordion before completing Activity 11 on the page that follows.

Though instructions are not always required, they can be helpful for screen reader users when there is non-standard keyboard navigation. In our case, we'll add a few words and assign them to the "instructions" variable in the default settings of the init() function for the carousel. The instructions will be rendered in its own <div> and referenced with aria-describedby a little later in the code.

We'll define a few attributes when the carousel is initialized: give it a role="region" to add it to the landmarks, add a tabindex to make it keyboard focusable, and reference the ID of the instructions <div> with aria-describedby. Add keyboard operability with .on('keydown') and a reference to the onKeyDown function, described below.

Screen reader users will not need the Next/Previous controls, so hide them. They will be using the Arrow keys instead, defined in the onKeyDown function further below.

Hide images from screen readers. Notice that the alt text for the images are defined in the HTML but left empty so it is not read in this case. Screen readers will read the figcaptions.

Add screen reader instructions by generating a <div> that contains the instruction text defined earlier and hide the <div> by default. The instructions are read when the carousel receives focus, and the aria-describedby attribute is dynamically added to reference the instructions.

Add an aria-live attribute to the stopTimer function. Set its value to polite so content updating in the live region announces when a screen reader is not reading elsewhere on the page. The content of the visible carousel panel is read automatically when it is in focus, manually navigating between panels with the Arrow keys.

Remove the live region when focus on the carousel is removed in the startTimer function. By doing so, the live region stops reading when the timer is reactivated onblur, and it does not interfere with the screen reader reading elsewhere on the page.

Hide the active slide from screen readers with aria-hidden="true". Then, make the next slide visible to screen readers with aria-hidden="false" in the gotoSlide function.

Adding Keyboard Operability

Add keyboard operations for the carousel, pulling keyboard events from ik_utils.js to use Left and Right arrows for moving between panels in the carousel, and the Esc key to exit the carousel and resume automatic rotation.

Accessible Carousel in Action

Watch the following video to see how ChromeVox interacts with a carousel. The carousel rotates automatically when focus is elsewhere on the page. When it receives focus, rotation stops, and navigation instructions are read. The Left and Right arrow keys are used to move manually between panels in the carousel while it has focus. The contents of each panel are read through a live region, dynamically added to the main container <div> when the carousel has focus. Using the Tab key while the carousel has focus sends focus to any focusable element within the panel that is in view, a link to the person who shared the photo in this case. Aim to have the carousel you update in the activity on the following page operate and announce like the one in the video.

Video: Accessible Carousel

A YouTube element has been excluded from this version of the text. You can view it online here: https://pressbooks.library.ryerson.ca/wafd/?p=362

Activity 11: Accessible Carousel

Accessible Carousel

Based on the Carousel details on the previous page, apply what you have learned to the associated activity files to make the carousel there accessible.

Files for this activity include:

- ❖ /carousel.html
- ❖ /assets/ik_carousel.js

Use the surroundings of the highlighted code on the previous page as a guide to find where the fixes should be applied. Repair the accessibility of the carousel by applying the highlighted code to the /assets/ik_carousel.js file.

Note: While we suggest using the highlighted code we've provided, you are free to come up with your own solutions provided they produce the expected results listed in the marking rubric below.

Test your updated carousel with ChromeVox to ensure each element described in the marking rubric below is functioning as suggested.

Requirements

When you have applied your changes and tested to ensure your carousel functions as described, submit the URL to your carousel.html file on your GitHub Pages site, to the file on the web server you are using to host your copy of the activity files, or a GitHack URL.

Grading Rubric

Criteria	Points
Instructions Provided Screen reader instructions are provided when carousel receives focus.	1.0 pts
Carousel Focusable Carousel panels are keyboard focusable.	1.0 pts

Criteria	Points
Carousel Navigation Navigate between panels with the Left and Right Arrow keys.	3.0 pts
Panels Read Aloud While the carousel has focus, each panel reads aloud when it comes into view.	2.0 pts
Manual while in Focus When in focus, or while a mouse pointer is hovering over the carousel, panels rotate manually only.	2.0 pts
Rotate when No Focus When the carousel is not in focus, panels rotate automatically.	1.0 pts
Total Points:	10.0

6

Interactive WAI-ARIA (Advanced)

Menu Bars

Menu bars are typically presented horizontally across the top of a website or web application. They contain links to key areas of the website or application. They function as toggles that open submenus or function as both links and toggles. Menu bars remain in view across the entire website or application.

Roles, states, and properties used in a menu bar

- aria-hidden = [true|false]
- role = "menubar"
- role = "menu"
- role = "menuitem"
- aria-labelledby = "[instruction div id]"
- aria-label = [link text]
- tabindex = [0 | -1]
- aria-haspopup = "true"
- aria-expanded = "[true|false]"
- aria-selected = "[true|false]"

Suggested Reading: For more about accessible menus, see WAI-ARIA Best Practice 1.1: Menus or Menu Bar.

The following JSFiddle presents a typical menu bar widget with a variety of sub menus. Review the JavaScript and HTML markup. Test the menu bar presented under the Result tab with ChromeVox to understand how it functions without any accessibility features added. You can work in JSFiddle itself by clicking the "Edit in JSFiddle" link at the top, right-hand side, copying the accessibility/WAI-ARIA code described below to fix the accessibility of the menu bar before completing Activity 12 on the page that follows.

First, provide some instructions on how to use the menu with a keyboard and add them to the default options.

Hide the instructions from screen readers until needed, adding aria-hidden="true" to the instructions <div> defined when the menu is initialized.

Add role="menubar" to the top level <ul> in the menu. Make that <ul> keyboard focusable with tabindex="0", so it reads the instructions while in focus and referenced with aria-labelledby.

For all the menu items in the menu bar that have submenus, add role="menu" to their <ul> and hide them by default using aria-hidden="true". This can be located after the $elem.find('ul:eq(0)') block presented immediately above.

Hide the links in the menu items from screen readers by default using tabindex="-1" and setting aria-hidden="true".

Set up the menu items throughout the menu using role="menuitem". Also, remove keyboard access by default with tabindex="-1". Next, label each menu item with the text of the associated link using aria-label="[$link.text]".

For each of the menu items that has a submenu, add aria-haspopup="true" to announce the presence of the submenu, and set its default state to "collapsed" by adding aria-expanded="false".

When a menu item is marked selected, also add aria-selected="true" and add keyboard access back to the menu item with tabindex="0".

Add keyboard access back to menu items using tabindex="0".

Reference the keyboard access class, where mouse events are defined in the on Key Down function, described below.

In the show Sub Menu function, add aria-expanded="true" submenus when they are expanded, remove keyboard access from the submenu container with tabindex="-1". Then, make the submenu visible with aria-hidden="false".

In the hide Sub Menu function, set aria-expanded="false", hide submenus with aria-hidden="true", and remove keyboard access with tabindex="-1" when a submenu is closed.

When the collapse All function is called, to collapse any open menus, reverse all attributes defining the element as open, reverting to aria-hidden="true", aria-expanded="false" and re-adding keyboard access with tabindex="0" so it can be opened again.

Adding Keyboard Operability

Menu bar keyboard functionality can be complex, particularly with large menus with multiple levels of submenus, and they can include redundant keys that perform the same function. The W3C defines suggested keyboard interaction for a menu bar as follows:

Menu Bar Keyboard Interaction

This description of keyboard behaviours assumes the following:

- ❖ A horizontal menubar containing several menuitem elements.
- ❖ All items in the menubar have child submenus that contain multiple vertically arranged items.
- ❖ Some of the menuitem elements in the submenus have child submenus with items that are also vertically arranged.

When reading the following descriptions, also keep in mind these items:

- ❖ Focusable elements, which may have role menuitem, menuitemradio, or menuitem check box, are referred to as items.
- ❖ If a behaviour applies to only certain types of items, e.g., menuitem elements, the specific role name is used.
- ❖ Submenus, also known as pop-up menus, are elements with role menu.
- ❖ Except where noted, menus opened from a menu button behave the same as menus opened from a menu bar.
- ❖ When a menu opens, or when a menubar receives focus, keyboard focus is placed on the first item. All items are focusable as described in 5.6 Keyboard Navigation Inside Components.

Enter:

- ❖ When focus is on a menuitem that has a submenu, opens the submenu and places focus on its first item.
- ❖ Otherwise, activates the item and closes the menu.

Space:

- ❖ **(Optional):** When focus is on a menuitemcheckbox, changes the state without closing the menu.

- **(Optional):** When focus is on a menuitemradio that is not checked, without closing the menu, checks the focused menuitemradio and unchecks any other checked menuitemradio element in the same group.
- **(Optional):** When focus is on a menuitem that has a submenu, opens the submenu and places focus on its first item.
- **(Optional):** When focus is on a menuitem that does not have a submenu, activates the menuitem and closes the menu.

Down Arrow:

- When focus is on a menuitem in a menubar, opens its submenu and places focus on the first item in the submenu.
- When focus is in a menu, moves focus to the next item, optionally wrapping from the last to the first.

Up Arrow:

- When focus is in a menu, moves focus to the previous item, optionally wrapping from the first to the last.
- **(Optional):** When focus is on a menuitem in a menubar, opens its submenu and places focus on the last item in the submenu.

Right Arrow:

- When focus is in a menubar, moves focus to the next item, optionally wrapping from the last to the first.
- When focus is in a menu and on a menuitem that has a submenu, opens the submenu and places focus on its first item.
- When focus is in a menu and on an item that does not have a submenu, performs the following 3 actions:
- Closes the submenu and any parent menus.
- Moves focus to the next menuitem in the menubar.
- **Either:** (Recommended) opens the submenu of that menuitem without moving focus into the submenu, or opens the submenu of that menuitem and places focus on the first item in the submenu.

Note that if the menubar were not present, e.g., the menus were opened from a menubutton, Right Arrow would not do anything when focus is on an item that does not have a submenu.

Left Arrow:

- When focus is in a menubar, moves focus to the previous item, optionally wrapping from the last to the first.
- When focus is in a submenu of an item in a menu, closes the submenu and returns focus to the parent menuitem.
- When focus is in a submenu of an item in a menubar, performs the following 3 actions:
  - Closes the submenu.
  - Moves focus to the previous menuitem in the menubar.
- **Either:** (Recommended) opens the submenu of that menuitem without moving focus into the submenu, or opens the submenu of that menuitem and places focus on the first item in the submenu.
- **Home:** If arrow key wrapping is not supported, moves focus to the first item in the current menu or menubar.
- **End:** If arrow key wrapping is not supported, moves focus to the last item in the current menu or menubar.
- **Any key that corresponds to a printable character (Optional):** Move focus to the next menu item in the current menu whose label begins with that printable character.
- **Escape:** Close the menu that contains focus and return focus to the element or context, e.g., menu button or parent menuitem, from which the menu was opened.
- **Tab:** Moves focus to the next element in the tab sequence, and if the item that had focus is not in a menubar, closes its menu and all open parent menu containers.

Shift + Tab: Moves focus to the previous element in the tab sequence, and if the item that had focus is not in a menubar, closes its menu and all open parent menu containers.

Note:

- Disabled menu items are focusable but cannot be activated.
- A separator in a menu is not focusable or interactive.
- If a menu is opened or a menu bar receives focus as a result of a context action, Esc or Enter may return focus to the invoking context. For example, a rich text editor may have a menu bar that receives focus when a shortcut key, e.g., Alt+F10, is pressed while editing. In this case, pressing Esc or activating a command from the menu may return focus to the editor.

- ❖ Although it is recommended that authors avoid doing so, some implementations of navigation menu bars may have menuitem elements that both perform a function and open a submenu. In such implementations, Enter and Space bar perform a navigation function, e.g., load new content, while Down Arrow, in a horizontal menu bar, opens the submenu associated with that same menuitem.
- ❖ When items in a menubar are arranged vertically and items in menu containers are arranged horizontally:
- ❖ Down Arrow performs as Right Arrow is described above, and vice versa.
- ❖ Up Arrow performs as Left Arrow is described above, and vice versa.

Source: W3C WAI-ARIA 1.1 Authoring Practices

Here we have implemented a subset of the keyboard interaction W3C recommends in an onKeyDown() function that is called when event handlers are set up for menu items. These keys include Left and Right arrows, Up and Down arrows, the Space bar and Enter keys, and Tab and Esc keys. Copy the following function into the ik_menu.js file, near the end, to add keyboard operability to the menu.

Accessible Menu Bar in Action

Watch the following video showing ChromeVox interacting with a menu bar. The Tab key is used to navigate into the menu bar, to the first menu item, and to exit the menu bar. Left and Right arrow keys are used to move across the top level menu items. Up and Down arrows are used to move into and out of a submenu and to move between menu items in a submenu. The Space bar or Enter key are used to activate a menu item. The Esc key closes the current submenu. Aim to have the menu bar you update in the activity on the next page operate and announce itself like the one in the video.

Video: Accessible Menu Bar

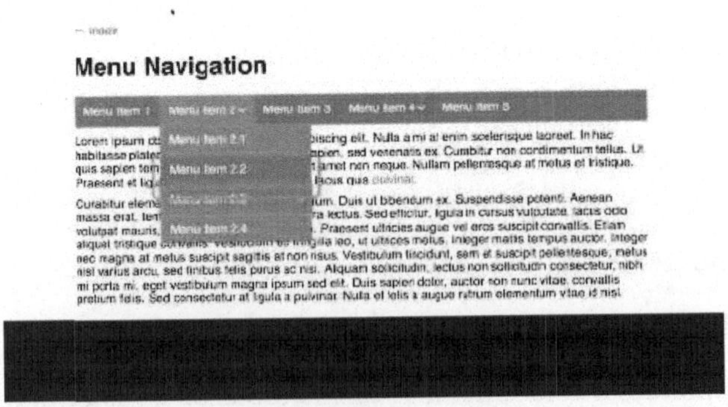

A YouTube element has been excluded from this version of the text. You can view it online here: https://pressbooks.library.ryerson.ca/wafd/?p=368

Activity 12: Accessible Menu Bar

Accessible Menu Bar

Based on the Menu bar details on the previous page, apply what you have learned to the associated activity files to make the menu there accessible.

Files for this activity include:

- /menu.html
- /assets/ik_menu.js

Use the surroundings of the highlighted code on the previous page as a guide to find where the fixes should be applied. Repair the accessibility of the menu bar by applying the highlighted code to the /assets/ik_menu.js file.

Note: While we suggest using the highlighted code we've provided, you are free to come up with your own solutions provided they produce the expected results listed in the marking rubric below.

Test your updated menu bar with Chrome Vox to ensure each element described in the marking rubric below is functioning as suggested.

Requirements

When you have applied your changes and tested to be sure your menu bar functions as described, submit the URL to your menu. html file on your GitHub Pages site, to the file on the web server you are using to host your copy of the activity files, or a GitHack URL.

Grading Rubric

Criteria	Points
Instructions Provided: Instructions are announced on how to use the menu bar with a keyboard, when the menu bar first receives focus.	1.0 pts
Menu Bar Semantics: List item semantics are replaced with menu semantics.	2.0 pts
Submenus Announced: When a menu item with a submenu receives focus, the presence of a submenu is announced.	2.0 pts
Focus Control: Only elements of the menu bar that are in view are able to receive focus.	2.0 pts
Keyboard Operable: As described in Adding Keyboard Operability for a menu bar, the menu bar functions using a keyboard (and mouse).	3.0 pts
Total Points:	10.0

Tree Menus

Tree menus often have the same underlying HTML structure as a menu bar, but rather than being arranged in a horizontal layout, they tend to be arranged vertically.

WAI-ARIA roles, states, and properties used in a tree menu

- tabindex = [0 | -1]
- aria-labelledby = [instruction div id | title div id]
- aria-hidden = [true | false]
- role = “tree”
- role = “treeitem”
- role = “presentation”
- aria-level = [number of parent ULs]
- aria-setsize = [number of LIs in a level]
- aria-posinset = [position of each LI in a set]
- aria-expanded = [true | false]
- aria-selected = [true | false]

Suggested Reading: For more about accessible tree menus, see WAI-ARIA 1.1 Authoring Practices 1.1: Tree View

The following JSFiddle presents a typical tree menu widget with a few submenus. Review the JavaScript and HTML markup. Test the tree menu presented under the

Result tab with ChromeVox to understand how it functions without any accessibility features added. You can work in JSFiddle itself by clicking "Edit in JSFiddle" at the top, right-hand side, copying the accessibility/WAI-ARIA code described below to fix the accessibility of the tree menu before completing Activity 13 on the page that follows.

First, define instructions on using the tree menu with a keyboard.

Within the init() function add keyboard focus to the tree container by applying tabindex="0" to it, and label the container with the instructions created above, which gets read by screen readers when the menu initially receives focus.

Within the init() function, hide the instructions <div> from screen readers by default by setting aria-hidden="true" when the tree menu is initialized.

Within the init() function replace the unordered list semantics with tree menu semantics using role="tree", and give it a title using aria-labelledby to reference the title defined in the default options.

Within the init() function, define menu items with role="treeitem", remove all keyboard access by default with tabindex="-1", set the number of levels in the tree based on the number of parent ULs with aria-level=[number of ULs], set the number of tree items on a given level with aria-setsize="[number of LIs in a UL]", and finally define the position of each tree item within a level using aria-posinset="[child LI index]".

Within the init() function, if a tree item has a submenu UL that has been opened, set aria-expanded="true", otherwise set aria-expanded="false".

Within the init() function, for each tree item use the text of the associated span element as its label. To ensure both the label and the contents of the span element are not both read, assign role="presentation" to the span.

Within the init() function, where mouse onclick functionality is used, provide equivalent keydown functionality, here referencing the onKeyDown function, shown below, that defines the keys to operate the menu.

Within the init() function, right after adding keydown operability, make the first item in the tree menu focusable by adding tabindex="0" to the first li.

Within the selectItem() function, set up a roving tabindex, while at the same time applying aria-selected=[true | false] when tree items receive or lose focus.

In the toggleSubmenu() function, announce the state of submenus to the screen reader by toggling the aria-expanded=[true | false] attribute when a menu is opened or closed.

Adding Keyboard Operability

Much like the menu bar described in the previous activity, keyboard operability for a tree menu can be complex, with various operations using multiple key strokes to perform the same function. W3C describes potential keyboard operation in the WAI-ARIA Authoring Practices 1.1, reproduced below.

Tree Menu Keyboard Interaction

For a vertically oriented tree:

- **When a single-select tree receives focus:**
  - If none of the nodes are selected before the tree receives focus, focus is set on the first node.
  - If a node is selected before the tree receives focus, focus is set on the selected node.
- **When a multi-select tree receives focus:**
  - If none of the nodes are selected before the tree receives focus, focus is set on the first node.
  - If one or more nodes are selected before the tree receives focus, focus is set on the first selected node.
- **Right Arrow:**
  - When focus is on a closed node, opens the node; focus does not move.
  - When focus is on a open node, moves focus to the first child node.
  - When focus is on an end node, does nothing.
- **Left Arrow:**
  - When focus is on an open node, closes the node.
  - When focus is on a child node that is also either an end node or a closed node, moves focus to its parent node.
  - When focus is on a root node that is also either an end node or a closed node, does nothing.
- **Down Arrow:** Moves focus to the next node that is focusable without opening or closing a node.
- **Up Arrow:** Moves focus to the previous node that is focusable without opening or closing a node.

- **Home:** Moves focus to the first node in the tree without opening or closing a node.
- **End:** Moves focus to the last node in the tree that is focusable without opening a node.
- **Enter:** Activates a node, i.e., performs its default action. For parent nodes, one possible default action is to open or close the node. In single-select trees where selection does not follow focus (see note below), the default action is typically to select the focused node.
- Type-ahead is recommended for all trees, especially for trees with more than 7 root nodes:
  - **Type a character:** focus moves to the next node with a name that starts with the typed character.
  - **Type multiple characters in rapid succession:** focus moves to the next node with a name that starts with the string of characters typed.
- *** (Optional):** Expands all siblings that are at the same level as the current node.
- **Selection in multi-select trees:** Authors may implement either of two interaction models to support multiple selection: a recommended model that does not require the user to hold a modifier key, such as Shift or Ctrl, while navigating the list or an alternative model that does require modifier keys to be held while navigating in order to avoid losing selection states.
  - **Recommended selection model–** holding a modifier key while moving focus is not necessary:
    - **Space**: Toggles the selection state of the focused node.
    - **Shift + Down Arrow (Optional):** Moves focus to and toggles the selection state of the next node.
    - **Shift + Up Arrow (Optional):** Moves focus to and toggles the selection state of the previous node.
    - **Shift + Space (Optional):** Selects contiguous nodes from the last selected node to the current node.
    - **Ctrl + Shift + Home (Optional)**: Selects the node with focus and all nodes up to the first node.
    - **Ctrl + Shift + End (Optional):** Selects the node with focus and all nodes down to the last node.
    - **Ctrl + A (Optional):** Selects all nodes in the tree. Optionally, if all nodes are selected, it can also unselect all nodes.

- Alternative selection model – moving focus without holding the Shift or Ctrl modifier unselects all selected nodes except for the focused node:
  - **Shift + Down Arrow:** Moves focus to and toggles the selection state of the next node.
  - **Shift + Up Arrow:** Moves focus to and toggles the selection state of the previous node.
  - **Ctrl + Down Arrow:** Without changing the selection state, moves focus to the next node.
  - **Ctrl + Up Arrow:** Without changing the selection state, moves focus to the previous node.
  - **Ctrl + Space:** Toggles the selection state of the focused node.
  - **Shift + Space (Optional):** Selects contiguous nodes from the most recently selected node to the current node.
  - **Ctrl + Shift + Home (Optional):** Selects the node with focus and all nodes up to the first node.
  - **Ctrl + Shift + End (Optional):** Selects the node with focus and all nodes down to the last node.
  - **Ctrl + A (Optional):** Selects all nodes in the tree. Optionally, if all nodes are selected, it can also unselect all nodes.

Note:

- DOM focus (the active element) is functionally distinct from the selected state. For more details, see this description of differences between focus and selection.
- The tree role supports the aria-activedescendant property, which provides an alternative to moving DOM focus among treeitem elements when implementing keyboard navigation. For details, see Managing Focus in Composites Using aria-activedescendant.
- In a single-select tree, moving focus may optionally unselect the previously selected node and select the newly focused node. This model of selection is known as "selection follows focus". Having selection follow focus can be very helpful in some circumstances and can severely degrade accessibility in others. For additional guidance, see Deciding When to Make Selection Automatically Follow Focus.
- If selecting or unselecting all nodes is an important function, implementing separate controls for these actions, such as buttons for "Select All" and "Unselect All", significantly improves accessibility.

If the nodes in a tree are arranged horizontally:

- Down Arrow performs as Right Arrow is described above and vice versa.
- Up Arrow performs as Left Arrow is described above and vice versa.

Source: WAI-ARIA Authoring Practices 1.1

For the tree menu created here, we've added in basic keyboard operability. Keyboard operation includes: Up and Down, and Left and Right Arrows for navigating within the tree, and the Enter or Space bar keys to toggle submenus open or closed. The Tab key by default enters and exits the tree menu and does not need to be defined as part of the keyboard operability of the tree menu.

Accessible Tree Menu in Action

Watch the following video showing ChromeVox interacting with a tree menu. The Tab key is used to navigate into the tree menu, to the first tree item, and to exit the tree menu. The Up and Down arrows are used to move between tree items. The Space bar or Enter key are used to expand and collapse a tree item with a submenu. When a submenu is opened, focus moves to the first tree item in the menu. Aim to have the tree menu you update in Activity 13 operate and announce itself like the one in the video.

Video: Accessible Tree Menu

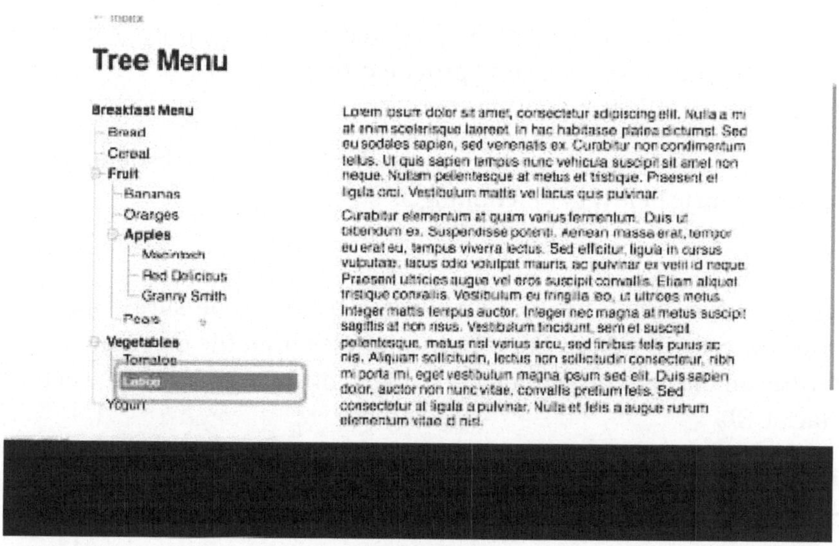

A YouTube element has been excluded from this version of the text. You can view it online here: https://pressbooks.library.ryerson.ca/wafd/?p=374

Activity 13: Accessible Tree Navigation

Based on the Tree Menu details on the previous page, apply what you have learned to the associated activity files to make the tree menu there accessible.

Files for this activity include:

- /tree.html
- /assets/ik_treemenu.js

Use the surroundings of the highlighted code on the previous page as a guide to find where the fixes should be applied. Repair the accessibility of the tree menu by applying the highlighted code to the /assets/ik_treemenu.js file.

Note: While we suggest using the highlighted code we've provided, you are free to come up with your own solutions provided they produce the expected results listed in the marking rubric below.

Test your updated tree menu with ChromeVox to ensure each element described in the marking rubric below is functioning as suggested.

Requirements

When you have applied your changes and tested to be sure your tree menu functions as described, submit the URL to your tree.html file on your GitHub Pages site, to the file on the web server you are using to host your copy of the activity files, or a GitHack URL.

Grading Rubric

Criteria	Points
Instructions Provided: When the tree menu receives focus, instructions are announced on how to use the menu with a keyboard.	1.0 pts
Tree Menu Semantics: When navigating through the tree menu with a keyboard, elements are announced with tree menu semantics.	2.0 pts

Criteria	Points
Tree Submenus: When a tree menu item with a submenu receive focus, the submenu state is announced as expanded when open or collapsed when closed.	2.0 pts
Focus Control: Only elements of the tree menu that are in view are able to receive focus.	2.0 pts
Keyboard Operable: Tree menu functions with a keyboard as described in Adding Keyboard Operability for tree menus.	3.0 pts
Total Points:	10.0

Sortable Lists

One of the more common types of widgets that present barriers for screen reader users are drag and drop features. These can be set up in a grid, where draggable items can be rearranged horizontally or vertically by clicking on an item and moving it to a new position in the grid. A drag and drop may also be a sortable list, where items in a list can be dragged vertically to perhaps position the more important list items near the top of the list. For drag and drop elements you may come across on the Web today, the vast majority only function with a mouse, making them inaccessible to many people who rely on a keyboard to navigate. Here, we will look at a sortable list, and the WAI-ARIA and associated keyboard operability required to make that list sortable while using only a screen reader and a keyboard.

Role, states, and properties used in a sortable list

- role = "list"
- role = "listitem"
- tabindex = "[0 | -1]"
- aria-labelledby = "[instruction div id]"
- aria-hidden = "[true | false]"

Suggested Reading: 4 Major Patterns for Accessible Drag and Drop

The following JSFiddle presents a typical sortable list widget. Review the JavaScript and HTML markup, and test the list presented under the Result tab with ChromeVox to understand how it functions without any accessibility features added. You can work in JSFiddle itself by clicking "Edit in JSFiddle" at the top, right-hand side, copying the accessibility/WAI-ARIA code described below to fix the accessibility of the menu bar before completing Activity 14 on the page that follows.

As usual, create instructions on using the sortable list with a keyboard. In this case, we also want to determine which modifier key to include in the instructions. For Mac, it will be the Command key, otherwise it will be the Control key. Here, the standard accesskey key commands will also work as the modifier and can potentially be described as well (e.g., Ctrl + Alt on Mac, or Ctrl on Windows).

Assign a redundant role="list" to the opening ul, make the ul keyboard focusable, and attach the instruction with aria-labelledby="[instruction div id]" so keyboard navigation details are announced when the list initially receives focus while using a screen reader.

Within the init() function, generate the <div> that will contain the instructions, and add aria-hidden="true" to hide it from screen readers by default.

In the items section of the init() function, where draggable is defined for each item in the list, add a redundant role="listitem", and generate a label for each item that describes the list item's current position and that that list item is "movable." Finally, set tabindex="0" on the first list item, and tabindex="-1" on the other list items in order to ensure a list item is focusable by default.

Where the draggable attributes are defined near the end of the init() function, attach a keydown reference to the onKeyDown() function to make the list draggable with a keyboard.

In the resetNumbering() function, update the label for moved items to reflect their new position in the list using aria-label = "[new position]".

Adding Keyboard Operability

Keyboard operation for a drag and drop sortable list is relatively simple, compared to the menu bar and tree menu. Essentially, only the Up and Down arrow keys are needed. The standard operating system modifier keys, typically used with tabindex (e.g., Crtl + Alt, Alt, or Ctrl), function as the modifier keys when using them in addition to the Up and Down arrows to grab, drag, and drop a list item.

The on Key Down() function for the sortable list presented below, defines just up and down arrow key operability, along with a roving tabindex. W3C has not yet created a best practice for authoring keyboard interaction for drag and drop elements.

Sortable List in Action

Watch the following video showing ChromeVox interacting with a sortable list. The Tab key is used to navigate into the list and to exit the list. The Up and Down arrows are used to move between list items. On a Mac, the Command key plus Up or Down arrow, selects a list item and moves it to a new location. On windows the Ctrl key is used instead of Command, along with the Up or Down arrow keys to move list items. Aim to have the sortable list you update in the activity on the next page operate and announce itself like the one in the video.

Video: Accessible Sortable List

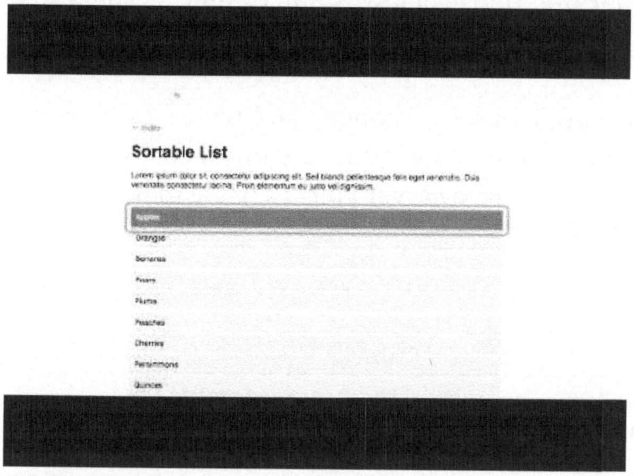

A YouTube element has been excluded from this version of the text. You can view it online here: https://pressbooks.library.ryerson.ca/wafd/?p=379

Activity 14: Accessible Sortable List

Based on the Sortable List details on the previous page, apply what you have learned to the associated activity files to make the sortable list there accessible.

Files for this activity include:

- /sortable.html
- /assets/ik_sortable.js

Use the surroundings of the highlighted code on the previous page as a guide to find where the fixes should be applied, Repair the accessibility of the sortable list by applying the highlighted code to the /assets/ik_sortable.js file.

Note: While we suggest using the highlighted code we've provided, you are free to come up with your own solutions provided they produce the expected results listed in the marking rubric below.

Test your updated sortable list with ChromeVox to ensure each element described in the marking rubric below is functioning as suggested.

Requirements

When you have applied your changes and tested to be sure your sortable list functions as described, submit the URL to your sortable.html file on your GitHub Pages site, to the file on the web server you are using to host your copy of the activity files, or a GitHack URL.

Grading Rubric

Criteria	Points
Instructions Provided: Instructions are announced on using the sortable list with a keyboard when it first receives focus.	1.0 pts
Movable List Items: When navigating through list items, their position is announced along with an indication they can be moved.	2.0 pts
List Items are Sortable: Using the keyboard operation described in Adding Keyboard Operability for sortable lists, list items can be moved without using a mouse.	3.0 pts
Moved position: When a list items is moved, its new position is announced.	4.0 pts
Total Points:	10.0

Content Recap

Unit 1 Summary

Unit 1 focused on getting started and providing the background information on the WAI-ARIA specification. The jQuery plugin being developed was also introduced, and access to the inaccessible versions of the widgets that make up the plugin, also known as the activity files, was provided on GitHub. You were also introduced to a MooTools WAI-ARIA library and another jQuery library that can also be used to quickly add WAI-ARIA to interactive web elements.

Though the focus here is on jQuery, the application of WAI-ARIA with other JavaScript frameworks will be quite similar. Developers are encouraged to apply what they learn via jQuery to other libraries they may be working with.

In Unit 1, you were also introduced to the ChromeVox screen reader. Though not a screen reader people who are blind would often use, ChromeVox is an ideal tool for developers to test accessibility in their day-to-day development work.

Unit 2 Summary

In Unit 2, a more detailed description of WAI-ARIA was provided, with a discussion of when and when not to use it; understanding WAI-ARIA roles, states, and properties; as well as differences between static and dynamic application of WAI-ARIA. Though some WAI-ARIA can be added directly to HTML as static attributes, in many cases WAI-ARIA is added dynamically as needed using JavaScript. We also looked at support across assistive technologies (AT) and web browsers. Currently (as of Novermber 2019), support is varied across these technologies but improving constantly.

We also introduced graceful degradation and progressive enhancement as development methods that can be employed to ensure that elements that may not yet be supported across all technologies have alternatives available as fallbacks, ensuring features are functional regardless of the technology being used. Despite the variation in support for WAI-ARIA, developers are encouraged to use it now, with the assumption that support for it will continue to improve over the coming years.

We also introduced LightHouse and aXe, two tools that can be used to validate WAI-ARIA to ensure it is being used correctly. These tools can be added to Chrome, along with ChromeVox (introduced in Unit 1), to have a collection of accessibility testing tools at your fingertips when developing for the Web. Finally the WAI-ARIA Taxonomy was introduced to help participants visualize the structure and relationships between WAI-ARIA roles, states, and properties.

Unit 3 Summary

In Unit 3, you built upon your understanding of WAI-ARIA with some practical implementations by looking at landmarks for implementing within page navigation for screen reader users, alerts and messages for providing easy access feedback, the new tabindex values 0 and -1 used to add keyboard access to elements that do not typically have keyboard access, and development of roving tabindexes that add and remove keyboard access as needed as users interact with a widget or application.

We also looked briefly at the WAI-ARIA application and presentation roles. The application role is typically used with embedded web applications where keyboard interaction needs to be intercepted so the application itself is being operated on rather than interacting with the assistive technology (AT) or the web browser. When using the application role, care must be taken to not disable other critical interactions with the web browser or AT and create unintended barriers when standard functionality becomes disabled.

The presentation role is used to hide elements from screen readers. They are typically used to hide table semantics when they are used for layout and to hide away images that are decorative. In the latter case, the presentation role works much like a null alt attribute would. Like the application role, care must be taken when using the presentation role to ensure meaningful information about the content is not being removed inadvertently.

Finally, we introduced live regions as a way to present updating information in web content. Typically, a screen reader processes the HTML of a page when it loads, and when content in the page changes, such as a newsfeed adding a new headline, they may not notice that change. Live regions are a way to make that updated information available to a screen reader, but care must be taken to ensure that information that updates frequently does not interfere with a screen reader's ability to read content elsewhere on the page.

Unit 4 Summary

In Unit 4 and the two units that follow, the focus moved to the practical implementation of WAI-ARIA, looking at specific interactions and the types of information that need to be available to assistive technologies to ensure these interactions are accessible to users of these AT.

In this unit, we looked specifically at:

- **Suggestion Boxes:** Instructions were provided on how to use the suggestion box, which provides suggested terms as letters are typed in, based on those letters. A live region was added to announce suggestions, and keyboard access was provided through the arrow keys scripted to navigate the suggestion list.
- **Tooltips:** When a parent element with a tooltip receives focus, the tooltip appears in a live region and reads out loud. When focus moves away, the tooltip disappears.
- **Progress Bars:** Instructions were provided on how to operate the progress bar with a keyboard to announce the status of the progress and indicate how far along progress is.

Unit 5 Summary

In Unit 5, the widgets got a little more complex. These included:

- **Sliders:** A slider bar and a slider thumb were created, minimum and maximum values were set for the slider bar, and an increment was set for the slider thumb, with each movement of the thumb moving a specific distance along the slider bar. Instructions were provided on how to operate the slider, with arrow keys used to move left and right across the slider bar, and Home and End keys used to move the slider thumb between the start and end of the slider bar.
- **Accordions:** Two types of accordion interactions were introduced: single or multiple accordion panels. They were each opened one at a time and opened or closed by toggling accordion headers with the Enter key or space bar. The

Tab key was used to navigate into an accordion, to navigate from one header to another, or to navigate from a header to its associated panel. Arrow keys were also used to navigate between accordion headers but not to their associated panels.

- **Tab Panels:** Much like accordions are used to conserve space, tab panels provide similar functionality, though typically content is arranged horizontally whereas accordions typically arrange content vertically. The Tab key is used to navigate into the tab panel's tabs, from tabs to their associated panels, and to exit the tab panel. The Left and Right Arrow keys are used to move between tabs, and when a panel has focus, Shift + Tab is used to return focus to the tab list. The semantics of the list used to create the tab panel are replaced with tab panel semantics.

- **Carousels:** Again, carousels are used to conserve space, presenting a series of slides or panels that contain images and text. A carousel typically rotates between panels automatically. When the Tab key is used to enter the carousel, automatic rotation stops, allowing users to spend as much time as they need to consume the information on each panel. The Left and Right Arrow keys are used to move between panels in the carousel. When the carousel has focus, a live region is created using the containing <div>, so as each slide comes into view its content is automatically read. When the Tab key is used to exit the carousel, the live region is removed and auto-rotation is restored. Removing the live region ensures the content of the slides does not continue to read out loud while the user is navigating other areas of the page.

Unit 6 Summary

In this final unit, the widgets got more complex yet.

- **Menu Bars:** Menu bars typically appear as a set of nested lists, with the top level list arranged horizontally across the top of a page and sublists acting as submenus. Specific menu bar and menu WAI-ARIA attributes were used to replace the list semantics with menu semantics, making them easier to understand when operating them with a screen reader. The Tab key is used to enter and exit the menu bar. Arrow keys are used to move between menu items, the space bar is used to open a submenu, and Esc is used to close an active submenu.

- **Tree Menu:** Tree menus often appear down the side of a page and include top-level topics and related subtopics that expand or contract with a toggle. Subtopics may open several levels deep. The Tab key is used to enter and exit the tree menu, and Up and Down Arrows are used to move between the menu items that are displayed. A roving tabindex is used to prevent focus on menu items that are not being displayed. When a menu item is accessed that has subtopics, the space bar or the Enter key can be used to toggle submenus open or closed.

When a menu item with a submenu receives focus, its state — expanded or collapsed — is announced by the screen reader. At any time while in the tree menu, pressing the Tab key exits the menu.

- **Sortable List:** The sortable list is a type of drag and drop widget. Many of these currently found on the Web are difficult or impossible to use with a keyboard alone, making them inaccessible to many users. The Tab key is used to enter and exit the list. Instructions are provided on how to operate the list using a keyboard. Up and Down Arrows are used to move up and down through the list. As list items receive focus, they announce as movable to indicate that they can be rearranged. Pressing Command, Alt + Ctrl, or just Alt — depending on the browser and operating system — along with the Up or Down Arrows, moves an item to an adjacent location in the list, announcing the new location for that item.

Web Accessibility for Developers Toolkit

Toolkit Items Collected

Toolkit: Provides useful tools and resources for your future reference.

- Join GitHub
- SourceTree
- GitHub Desktop
- jQuery UI Accessibility Enhancements
- Accessible MooTools Widgets
- WAI-ARIA Authoring Practices 1.1
- ARIA Techniques for WCAG 2.0
- Using WAI-ARIA
- ChromeVox Screen Reader
- ChromeVox_Key_Commands (Word)
- The ARIA Role Matrices
- WAI-ARIA Screen Reader Compatibility
- WAI-ARIA Browser Compatibility
- ARIA Alert Support
- User Agent Support Notes for ARIA Techniques
- W3C HTML Validator

- Chrome Developer Tools
- Lighthouse
- ARIA Validator
- aXe (for Chrome)
- aXe (for Firefox)
- Combobox
- Grid
- Listbox
- Menu or menu bar
- Radiogroup
- Tabs
- Toolbar
- Tree View

Index

Printed at Repro India Ltd.